BLACK AND PROUD

The story of an
iconic AFL photo

BLACK
AND
PROUD

Matthew Klugman
and Gary Osmond

NEWSOUTH

A NewSouth book

Published by
NewSouth Publishing
University of New South Wales Press Ltd
University of New South Wales
Sydney NSW 2052
AUSTRALIA
newsouthpublishing.com

National Library of Australia
Cataloguing-in-Publication entry
Author: Klugman, Matthew, 1975–, author.
Title: Black and Proud: The story of an iconic AFL photo / Matthew
    Klugman and Gary Osmond.
ISBN: 9781742234052 (paperback)
9781742241661 (ePub/Kindle)
9781742246673 (ePDF)
Notes: Includes index.
Subjects: Winmar, Nicky – Pictorial works. / Australian Football League. /
    St. Kilda Football Club. / Collingwood Football Club. / Football fans –
    Social aspects – Australia. / Athletes, Aboriginal Australian. / Australian
    football – Tournaments. / Discrimination in sports – Australia. / Race
    discrimination – Australia.
Other Authors/Contributors: Osmond, Gary, author.
Dewey Number: 796.336

Design Di Quick
Cover design Xou Creative
Cover image Wayne Ludbey/Fairfax Syndication

ISEAL
INSTITUTE OF SPORT,
EXERCISE AND ACTIVE LIVING

Contents

Sport has the power to change the world ...
to inspire ...
to unite people in a way that little else can.
Nelson Mandela

That was the AFL's Rosa Parks moment.
Steve Hawke

Kids at the Rumbalara Football & Netball Club in Shepparton, Victoria, re-enact Nicky Winmar's gesture, 2008.

We use the word 'Indigenous' to include both Aboriginal and Torres Strait Islander people collectively, and prefer 'Aboriginal' over 'Aborigine' except where cited in the original source. We also employ the collective terms used by specific Indigenous peoples such as 'Koori', 'Noongar', 'Nunga' and 'Yolngu'. Many of the insults detailed in this book are deeply offensive but we think it is vital to engage with the painful, as well as inspiring, aspects of our history.

Prologue

Life had hardened Charlie McAdam. Taken screaming and kicking from his mother before his seventh birthday, he survived the infamous Moola Bulla station that was supposed to 'civilise' him, stealing swill from pigs to ease his hunger and enduring floggings that left him unable to walk. By the age of thirteen Charlie was working as a stockman, and after that he experienced the bruises and fears of someone boxing for money, not love. He'd been paid to break in horses and steers, empty out toilets, drive trucks, reinforce pipes and assist Aboriginal people in need of legal aid. Yet even in his late fifties the crowd at Victoria Park made eyes that had seen so much pain run wet with tears.

It happened on 17 April 1993. Charlie was at Collingwood's home ground for the first time to see his son, Gilbert, play for St Kilda. Victoria Park had a deserved reputation as the most feral real estate in all of football. Tens of thousands of men, women and children would cram into the ground, packing the 'outer' like matches in a box. Kids perched on milk crates or craned to catch the on-field action around the legs of men who pissed in beer cans rather than force a path to the toilets through the crush and congestion. At the ground's Yarra end, where visiting supporters congregated for comfort and safety amid the sea of black-and-white fanatics, it was a rare day when the lavatories were not overflowing by half time and the air ripe with the stink of urine. Victoria Park was that sort of place.

When the game began, the Pies barrackers roared in unison, baying for blood. Thoughts of ancient Rome's Colosseum sprang readily to mind, and few blood-hungry Collingwood fanatics would have objected to the comparison. It was footy at its most tribal. And on this day the battle rage of the Magpie horde was directed most often at St Kilda's two Aboriginal players, Gilbert McAdam and Nicky Winmar.

Wedged among Collingwood barrackers in the notorious outer, Charlie saw Gilbert and Nicky carve up the Pies. Gilbert kicked four of the Saints' first five goals, Nicky continually drove the Saints forward, and both were excelling at the hard things, tackling and pressuring the Magpie players with fierce intensity. But Charlie's pleasure in their deeds was repeatedly crushed by the rude, racist invective filling the air around him.

Cries of 'petrol sniffers', 'abos', 'coons' were flung like daggers from behind the fence, an aural accompaniment to the reek of the outer's clogged toilets and every bit as foul. 'Shoot him! He is only a black', screamed one Magpies supporter. Others regularly branded Winmar and McAdam as 'niggers' and 'boongs' or gibbered like monkeys. The atmosphere was poisonous with hate, the racial insults relentless. 'Black' was used as if it were a grave insult. There are many foul slurs and epithets in the thick lexicon of abuse reserved for Indigenous Australians. Few were not uttered that day.

Charlie McAdam didn't want to believe what he was witnessing. This was 1993, International Year of the World's Indigenous People, but the clock at Victoria Park was stuck on an earlier, uglier time. Paul Keating had called for change with his famous Redfern Address just a few months before. The Northern Territory station where Charlie was once head stockman had been given back to its traditional owners several days later. There was a broad social movement against racism in Australia, and these advances reflected its growing strength. Yet the white faces in the crowd did not seem surprised, let alone offended, by the abuse directed at McAdam's son and Winmar. The racism and venom appeared part and parcel of just another day at the footy.

Charlie McAdam couldn't block it out, turn the deaf ear. He had stared into racism's face from his earliest years, but this was too much. It should have been a father's proudest moment, watching his boy give the Pies a lesson in the footy arts of crumbing, baulking, snapping and tackling.

But it was too much to bear, even for him. He left the game with tears streaming down his face. 'I just couldn't stomach it', Charlie explained later. 'I was so upset and disappointed. I just couldn't stand this abuse.'

Photographers Wayne Ludbey of the *Age* and John Feder from the rival *Herald-Sun* could have told Charlie there was nothing unusual about what he had seen and heard. Crouched over their cameras at the boundary line watching the play unfold, both Ludbey and Feder had recently become conscious of this appalling aspect of footy culture. Neither knew what to do about it. Instead they tried to block it out and focus on the game.

Back at his hotel, Charlie listened to the rest of the game on the radio. He was livid with a fury made worse by a lifetime's bitter wisdom of what it meant to be a black man in a white world. That anger was something you just had to live with, learn to let it roll over you and off you, something you dismissed in the end with a resigned and frustrated acknowledgment that 'you can't do anything about it'.

On this occasion, however, Charlie McAdam was wrong. Back at Victoria Park something was about to be done. Gilbert and Nicky responded to the hatred by driving St Kilda to their first victory at Victoria Park in seventeen years. It was the biggest upset of the young season, but the game's greatest moment was yet to come.

When the final siren sounded, Ludbey and Feder kept their eyes on the pair, hoping for the photo that would tell the story of the game. Each saw Winmar raise his arms and turn around in a circle like a triumphant fighter saluting a hostile crowd. Then Nicky reacted to yet another venomous comment from a Magpies fan. Turning to face the Collingwood barrackers, he lifted his jumper, pointed to his stomach and said the words that reverberated throughout Australia:

'I'm black and I'm proud to be black.'

Listening to the call of the game in his hotel room – there were no live TV broadcasts in those days – Charlie McAdam couldn't see what was happening. Like the radio commentators, television cameras and newspaper journalists, he missed Winmar's act. He would soon see it, however, as would all of Australia, for both Ludbey and Feder had captured it on film.

Published the next day, both images were searing. Winmar stands tall, his flawless physique exposed by the lifted jumper, his finger pointing at his skin, all the while gazing defiantly at the crowd. The pose is at once public and intimate, a pronouncement of pride in the form of an open challenge.

The photos of Winmar's grand gesture would help change a nation. Plenty of protests had preceded Winmar's act, but sport reaches into a part of culture that the courts and politicians struggle to access. Not only did the photos taken by Ludbey and Feder focus the Australian Football League's attention on racism within the sport, they

5

became an enduring symbol of all Australia's rocky race relations. Twenty years later, the images continue to be printed and reprinted, spawning works that grace art galleries and inner-city walls turned with a spray-can's flourish into proud reminders of the moment when Nicky Winmar proclaimed 'Enough!'

. . . . . .

Like many Australians, we had long been fascinated by the power and resonance of Nicky Winmar's gesture. And because we are both migrants from nations with their own disturbing histories of racism, the images of Winmar's gesture held a particular pull for us. Matthew's homeland of South Africa was notorious for its system of apartheid, which classified, separated and discriminated against people on the basis of skin colour. The race relations of Canada have received less international attention, but Gary's childhood was marked by knowledge that Red Indian Lake in Newfoundland, where he'd played, was the site of the annihilation of the Beothuck people a century beforehand. Yet the white Australia we encountered in the 1980s seemed to have little sense of its own history of race relations. White South Africans were considered racist, white Australians and Canadians were not.

We saw this beginning to change. Newly arrived in Australia, Gary was struck by the protests against the bicentenary celebrations of 1988, and his Indigenous work colleagues brought an awareness of contemporary Indigenous lives and experiences, and the power of storytelling in survival. Meanwhile, Matthew was discovering that the histories of Australia and South Africa were more closely aligned than many Australians realised. Winmar's gesture pointed to difficult aspects of Australia's past as well as the present, and we both referred to it regularly while teaching students about the history of sport in Australia. And yet when we looked more closely at the history and impact of the image, we were struck by just how much the stories behind the moment and its image had been neglected. Words abound on Australian paintings and artwork, along with sports figures, yet somehow this most important of Australian sporting images has been taken for granted.

The image of Nicky Winmar pointing with defiant pride at his dark skin is familiar to most Australians, but the experiences that prompted him and Gilbert McAdam to seize the moment are not. Winmar himself is a household name through much of Australia yet almost no one knows of the appalling segregation he experienced while growing up. Perhaps if they weren't from the Northern Territory the McAdam family's extraordinary record of sporting achievement would be better known, but Gilbert's vital contribution was shaped as much by his encounters off the sporting field as on. And then there are the hidden battles that Wayne Ludbey and John Feder fought to see their photos published, and the burdens that the image brought.

In this book we return to the compelling moment of 17 April 1993, to the world before it, and to how the Winmar image provoked national debate and transformation. We journey back to an Australia where leading Indigenous footy players like Chris Lewis and Michael Long regularly received death threats, but a white kid could grow up in a comfortable Melbourne suburb with the innocent belief that Australia was a society largely free of racism.

We follow the journeys of Gilbert McAdam, Wayne Ludbey and John Feder, along with the complex path travelled by Nicky Winmar, who is forever reproduced in that instant and yet receives few public accolades for it. And we trace the transformation that the gesture initiated, from the way it laid bare the fault-lines of Australia's race relations to the way it set the scene for Michael Long's official complaint against racist abuse in 1995, and on to the 2013 incident where Adam Goodes, an Aboriginal player, stood tall in the face of racist remarks from a kid and the president of an Australian Football League (AFL) club.

But this is not just a tale of what has been gained. It is also the story of near misses, conflict, controversy and loss. There is the startling way the image of Winmar's gesture was almost passed over in the aftermath of the game, and the arguments that ensued between the photographers and their editors over images *and* words. Some photographs were neglected, such as Winmar blowing kisses to the crowd, while the photos that were published provoked revealing debates over both the 'right' of spectators to racially abuse players and whether Winmar was even referring in his gesture and words to the colour of his skin.

Then there are the questions of loss. Winmar made his statement at a fraught time for race relations. Questions of race were dominating the international as well as national news, with racial unrest in South Africa and the United States dominating headlines. The release from prison of Nelson Mandela and the police beating of Rodney King featured alongside newspaper reports of the Australian High Court's Mabo decision and Keating's Redfern Address. All lent power to the photograph of Winmar pointing at his skin, helping the image stand in for much broader issues of race in Australia and beyond. Yet perhaps the enduring appeal of Winmar's act also lies in the continued racism and discrimination faced by Australia's Indigenous peoples. His gesture not only retains a fresh edge, but also continues to represent a demand for change.

1

Agitating
for change

'I didn't think so
many people cared'

The best photos do more than freeze time. They capture
a moment and take us there, making witnesses of us all.
Here lies their power to inspire and transform – a power
tied to the stories, hopes, dreams and struggles that shape
our lives. Some touch only lightly upon these tales, flashing
their images briefly on cornea and cortex, where they burn
brightly and are then forgotten. Others become a vital part
of the story, and we return to them over and over again. The
image of Nicky Winmar pointing with pride to his skin is
one of these. It tells more than a single tale, reflects so much
more than a fleeting instant framed by a photographer's
eye. In that single, spontaneous gesture, Winmar melded
two fundamental Australian concerns – sport and race.

The story of the Winmar image begins with these two concerns, with Australia's proud passion for sport and its enduring discomfort regarding matters of race. The four characters at the heart of the photo's creation – Nicky Winmar, Gilbert McAdam, Wayne Ludbey and John Feder – were born during the tumultuous 1960s. All shared a love of Australian Rules football, but that was more or less where the common ground ended, for all were separated by very different heritages and experiences of race. It is a history that was largely hidden from the eyes of Ludbey and Feder, yet one to which Winmar and later McAdam were sentenced. Their different experiences of race would be brought defiantly into focus at Victoria Park to produce one of the most arresting and important statements of our time.

. . . . .

'Left-hand jab to the face now by Rose. A series of jabs, beautiful punches. A left to the head now by Harada. Jab by Rose. Hard right by Harada. Beautiful punch. And Rose counters with a beautiful left hook.' It was 26 February 1968, and Nicky Winmar was two years old, Gilbert McAdam not yet one, while Wayne Ludbey and John Feder were both five. As is often the case, Australians were behaving as if nothing was more important than a sporting contest. Only this time they were united in support of an Aboriginal man: Lionel Rose.

A brilliant young boxer, Rose had emerged from a life of hardship around Drouin in Victoria to win the Australian bantamweight title as an eighteen-year-old. A year later he knocked out Sydney's charismatic Rocky Gattellari in front of the harbour city fighter's own fans, then won them over by explaining, 'We wanted to win, but not this way'. Soon Rose was 'a sensation. Humble, self-effacing, gentle and thoughtful, he was a hero for all'.

Now the nineteen-year-old Rose was in Japan boxing against the legendary Japanese World Bantamweight Champion, Masahiko 'Fighting' Harada. A breathless Ron Casey called the fifteen-round fight into a phone from Tokyo. 'All across Australia that night people clung to radios as if the ringside announcer were Winston Churchill', reported *Sports Illustrated*. When an amazed Casey proclaimed Rose the winner, 'women wept' and 'men shouted'. Still a teenager, Lionel Rose was Australia's newest world champion.

Rose got the 'shock of his life' when he returned to Melbourne. This was the age of the Beatles, and Lionel was greeted like a rock star by hundreds of people at Essendon airport. They were the first of more than 100 000 people who came out to cheer him on that day. From the airport Rose was led to an open-topped car and driven to the Melbourne Town Hall through streets lined with people shouting their congratulations. Everyone wanted to shake his hand, to wish him well. Men, women and children cheered, sang and held up signs exclaiming 'Good on ya, Lionel'.

When the Victorian Premier and other dignitaries spoke to Rose inside the Town Hall, the huge crowd outside started chanting, 'We want Lionel, we want Lionel!' Photos of the moment captured the joyous mood. Thousands swarmed around Rose's car. Then, when the dignitaries finally finished chatting with him, Lionel appeared on the Town Hall balcony to rapturous applause. An overwhelmed Rose later confessed to the media that 'I didn't think so many people cared'.

Australia was now blind to colour, or so it seemed to many in the crowd that day. Not only was an Aboriginal man now the hero of all, they could also point to the referendum nine months earlier. In May 1967 an overwhelming 90.4 per cent of Australians had voted to recognise the original landowners in the rolls of citizens, and to also give the Commonwealth a mandate to create legislation for their benefit. It was the highest 'Yes' vote ever recorded in an Australian referendum and due cause for optimism. Yet this optimism would have been shaken if any of those celebrating the feats of Lionel Rose had been taken to the town where a young Nicky Winmar was growing up: Pingelly.

. . . . . .

Consult the web and the history of Pingelly looks like its main attraction. A small farming hamlet two hours from Perth in the Western Australian Wheatbelt, Pingelly is spruiked as an 'attractive town' that 'offers a rare insight into Western Australia's rich colonial heritage' and a region that 'mirrors the history and achievements of European settlement in Western Australia'. Back in the late 1960s, however, the 'rich colonial heritage' of Pingelly laid bare the failings, as well as achievements, of white settlement. The town itself was pleasant enough, with a grand hotel, a town hall, a courthouse, a bank, some churches, a hospital, a school, nice houses and a swimming pool. But when the breeze was blowing the wrong way a smell worse than Victoria Park on game-day would let you know that something was horribly wrong.

Follow the stench a kilometre out of town and you arrived at a collection of sheds with corrugated iron roofs and walls, and concrete floors. With no insulation and a gap between the walls and floors so 'the floor could be washed out', they seemed designed to make it worse inside than out. In summer they were unbearably hot, in winter awfully cold. Water leaked through the roofs when it rained, while wind blew in through the glassless windows. The sheds had no running water and the toilets and laundry were communal, though each shed had a bucket as well. It wasn't the buckets that caused the stink, though. That was due to the 'decrepit sewerage system' that frequently overflowed, filling the town's hospital with patients afflicted with gastroenteritis, among other ailments.

It was here that the local Noongar Aboriginal mob lived.

They were allowed in the main town, but only between the hours of 6 am and 6 pm or they'd spend the night locked up in a police cell. But even during daylight hours the Noongars weren't really welcome in Pingelly. You could be bashed for walking on the 'wrong side of the street', and taunted just for the colour of your skin. The men worked as farmhands, the women stayed at home to care for their children. It was a puzzling situation to grow up in. 'As young kids we didn't understand why we weren't living in the town', recalled Winmar.

This was the contradiction of Australia in the late 1960s. Lionel Rose was a hero of the nation in 1968 – the Melbourne Moomba King, Australian of the Year and recipient of an MBE – while many towns around the country seemed more reminiscent of South Africa or America's Deep South than of the colour-blind nation those voting in the 1967 referendum were hoping for. But how had it come to this? To answer this we have to go back to the history of Australia's race relations and the intriguing, powerful role sport played in this.

. . . . . .

'They seemed angry at our invasion of their territory.' So noted Captain James Stirling in his report of his expedition on the west coast of Australia in 1827. Stirling was surreptitiously exploring the Swan River in the hope of finding a suitable area for further British colonies in Australia (or New Holland as the continent was then called). His party of nineteen men had just encountered three armed Noongar men whose 'violent gestures' made him grateful for 'the space of water, which divided them from the boat'. A few days later Stirling felt threatened by a larger group of Noongar warriors who followed his boat along the river bank, making further 'violent gestures and great noise' and seemed likely to shower them with spears.

Despite these negative encounters, Stirling was already in love, or at least lust, with the land around the Swan River. Stirling's report to the Governor of New South Wales, Ralph Darling, was glowing. '[The] richness of the soil, the bright foliage of the Shrubs, the Majesty of the surrounding Trees, the abrupt and red-coloured banks of the river occasionally seen, and the view of the blue summits of the Mountains, from which we were not far distant, made the scenery around this spot as beautiful as anything of the kind I had ever witnessed.' The report convinced Darling to support the idea of a new settlement, but it took intense lobbying in London before the British Government agreed to establish a new colony at the mouth of the river. Founded on 18 June 1829, the Swan River Colony quickly led to the establishment of Perth and was soon renamed Western Australia, with James Stirling its first administrator.

Stirling hadn't forgotten about the 'angry' Noongars he'd encountered two years earlier. His official proclamation of the new colony noted that an emergency militia force would be established if 'hostile Native Tribes' attacked. But he also warned that anyone 'behaving in a fraudilent, cruel or felonious Manner towards the Aboriginees of the Country' would be 'tried for the Offence, as if the same had been committed against any other of His Majesty's Subjects'.

Stirling wanted to protect the Noongar from ill-treatment, yet at the same time he was taking their land away and giving it to the settlers. Even with the best of intentions it was a situation primed for disaster. The Noongars saw their best land given over to sheep and cattle, while the kangaroos and other animals they fed on were hunted on a mass scale for their meat and skins. And to top it all off they battled epidemics caused by European diseases against which they had no immunity. When the Noongars responded by killing and eating the sheep and cattle they were treated as thieves and punished accordingly. Faced with the escalating 'native problem', Stirling established a Superintendent of Natives in 1832 to 'protect and control' the Noongar population. Soon there was also a special mounted police corps to help deal with the Noongars.

. . . . . .

The difficulties that Stirling faced in Perth mirrored that of the other Australian colonies. Two Latin words summed up the general British attitude: *terra nullius*. The land was treated as if it 'belonged to no one', as if the Indigenous Australians were too primitive to either possess or manage the local terrain. In 1835, John Batman decided to act differently. The ruthless yet at times tender son of a man transported to Australia for receiving stolen goods, Batman had amassed thousands of acres in Van Diemen's Land (Tasmania), but with the island now fully grazed, he turned his sights to the nearby mainland. After his 1827 proposal to gain grazing pasture on the mainland was rejected, Batman set sail for the mouth of the Yarra and Maribyrnong rivers with a different plan in mind. He'd established the Port Phillip Association with other Tasmanian farmers and entrepreneurs, and hoped to follow the New Zealand practice of negotiating directly with the local landowners. On a waterway likely just a couple of kilometres upstream of the corroboree site that would become Victoria Park, Batman purportedly signed a treaty with Wurundjeri elders to perpetually lease about 2000 square kilometres of land around the Yarra River in return for yearly payments of tomahawks, clothes, blankets, knives, looking glasses, scissors and flour.

'I am the greatest landowner in the world', Batman announced on his return to Van Diemen's Land. But the representatives of the British Crown were unimpressed. To them, the land was owned by the British – Batman had no authority to negotiate with the Wurundjeri, and the Wurundjeri had no legal right to lease it. Indeed, anyone found in unauthorised possession of lands within the colony would be 'considered as trespassers', proclaimed the Governor of New South Wales, Richard Bourke, as he voided the treaty.

. . . . . .

It's hard to imagine now what it was like to live on your land one day, then be treated as a trespasser the next. The confusion was immense, the consequences drastic and frequently tragic. Across Australia the Aboriginal peoples resisted their dispossession while the British struggled to understand why the Indigenous Australians were unwilling or unable to follow the laws the newcomers brought with them. Within a few years, sometimes less, the settlements and colonies around Australia were marked by frontier battles and other forms of resistance.

John Batman might have been seeking to avoid these troubles, for he'd been party to the notorious 'Black War' in Van Diemen's Land where settlers and the traditional landholders battled each other for decades. Indeed, the land-hungry Batman had persuaded the Governor of Tasmania, George Arthur, to pay him with acreage in return for 'bringing in alive some of these much injured and unfortunate race of beings' for their own protection. Yet Batman did not always bring in alive the Aboriginals he captured. On one awful occasion Batman ordered his men to 'fire upon' a camp of Aboriginal people, then shot two of the wounded when they could not keep up. It says much about the attitudes of the day that Arthur could note that Batman 'has much slaughter to account for', while at another time praising him as 'one of the few who supposed that [Indigenous Tasmanians] might be influenced by kindness'.

. . . . . .

L ed by an inspiring warrior named Yagan, the dashing son of Noongar elder Midgegooroo, Nicky Winmar's forebears also fought fiercely against those who'd invaded their lands by establishing the colony at Swan River. A 'hero' or 'complete and untameable savage' depending on your perspective, the fearless Yagan excelled at spear throwing and led many Noongar raids for food and retribution in the early 1830s. When the settler George Fletcher Moore confronted Yagan about the murder of a white man, Yagan explained that white men had killed a black man. It was an indication that the act of revenge was sanctioned, even required, under Noongar law. When Moore pleaded with Yagan and his comrades to treat white men as his brothers instead of spearing them and their animals, Yagan gesticulated and spoke to him intensely. The language gap meant Moore was unsure exactly what Yagan said, but he believed it was along the lines of: 'You came to our country; you have driven us from our haunts, and disturbed us in our occupations: as we walk in our country we are fired upon by the white men; why should the white men treat us so?'

Moore was not alone in his sympathy for the Noongar population. Robert Lyon, a Scottish settler, saw some of the mistreatment of the local Noongars and became a passionate advocate of their rights. When Yagan and two companions were captured and sentenced to death in 1832, Lyon stepped in, arguing that they were freedom fighters like the Scottish hero William Wallace, and that they should be treated as prisoners of war. Governor Stirling relented, sending the men to nearby Carnac Island instead. Lyon also persuaded Stirling to let him spend time with the men. Upon seeing Lyon, Yagan wept with gratitude, and Lyon spent a month learning the Noongar language and developing ambitious plans for the men to become ambassadors and strike a treaty with the British Crown.

These lofty dreams were scuttled when Yagan and his companions escaped the island and returned to Perth. Lyon's calls for a treaty were ignored, while Yagan once again tried to uphold Noongar law. In March 1833 he negotiated with Captain Ellis, the Native Superintendent, to allow a corroboree, a ceremonial festival that enabled the Noongar to maintain their connection to the land. Yagan was master of ceremonies, a role he performed with 'infinite dignity and grace', as the Perth *Gazette* put it. Two months later, though, the *Gazette* was referring to Yagan as 'the daring villain we have too frequently had occasion to notice' and a 'bloodthirsty savage' for his role in a deadly revenge attack on some carts loaded with provisions. As the paper announced, there was now a £30 bounty 'for the body of the desperado, alive or dead'.

In July 1833, Yagan was murdered by two young shepherds whose boss he was on friendly terms with. The *Gazette* blasted it as a 'wild and treacherous act', 'not the heroic and courageous deed, which some unthinkingly have designated it'. The paper lamented that 'the savage' could 'draw no very favourable conclusions of our moral and physical superiority' from this deed. What followed added further insult to the act, for Yagan's body was skinned to gain his tribal markings, and his head lopped off and smoked for preservation before being dispatched to England where it was shown in the Liverpool Museum. It was an indication of the fascination the British held for Aboriginal Australians, but also of the way they treated them as objects, and body upon body was sent back for examination. Thirty years on it was live sporting bodies being sent to Britain to entertain the thousands yearning to see exotic Aboriginal people.

. . . . . .

There's something otherworldly about sport. We're enchanted by the intense contests performed before our eyes, the battles held on our behalf. The links of sport to war are obvious, but the other wellspring of religion is there too. Sporting fields somehow seem sacred spaces to many of us, deceptively simple places where different rules apply and everything seems possible, at least for a while. On the sporting field all are supposed to start as equals, to be separated only by the dictates of the talents they were born with and their willingness to play as if their lives depend on it.

The inherent goodness of sport is one of our central cultural tenets. Handed down for generations, this belief emerged from the British sporting revolution of the mid-1800s – a revolution whose effects still reverberate around the world. At the heart of it was the idea that sports like cricket and the football codes were the greatest tool for civilising boys and turning them into men of the highest character. The bestselling 1857 novel *Tom Brown's School Days* captured the mood perfectly, with the young hero learning 'discipline and reliance on one another' from the 'unselfish' games that merged the individual into a team where each boy 'doesn't play that he may win, but that his side may'.

As the fervour for these sports swept Australia, the colonists brought them to the Indigenous peoples they sought to manage. The hope was that British sports might help civilise them and also distract them from fighting for their land. It was a hope that set the scene for one of the most intriguing stories – and lingering silences – of Australia's sporting history.

In 1868 the first sporting team departed Australian shores. On board the boat was not the best the new Australians had to offer, but rather thirteen Aboriginal men from Victoria. They were embarking on the three-month trip to England to play a series of cricket matches after impressing pastoralist William Hayman, who had arranged for them to compete against white teams in Victoria and New South Wales. We don't know how willing the men were to tour England, how informed their consent was, or even really how they experienced the trip. As historian Sean Gorman notes, the silence around this is remarkable. What we do know is that they played valiantly, winning as many games as they lost (fourteen) and drawing the rest (nineteen). But the crowds were underwhelmed by these feats because the tourists seemed too normal. As popular British science writer the Reverend JG Wood noted, 'there was nothing remarkable about them, and in fact they seemed to be very ordinary persons indeed'. Instead, people flocked to see the performances on the last afternoon of each match when the Aboriginal men would exhibit their amazing skills with boomerangs and spears while dressed and painted in traditional fashion.

Mainstream scientists of the time like JG Wood believed in a hierarchy of races – white people were the most evolved, while those with the darkest skin were relics of the Stone Age and doomed to extinction, hence the desire to see the Aboriginal cricketers showcase their 'native' skills while their people still walked the earth. The Aboriginal men appeared to enjoy the performances as well, with Wood noting 'they walked with a proud elastic step that contrasted strangely with their former gait'. Yet the cricket skills of players like Johnny Mullagh and Johnny Cuzens were also impressive enough for one of their opponents, William South Norton, to lament that 'but for the fact that the race is dying out fast, more Mullaghs and Cuzenses would have been trained in the Colony'. There was a hint then that English sports might offer a chance for Indigenous Australians to be considered on their general (rather than racial) merits, but the hold of the racial science was too strong.

Nearly 50 years later, in 1914, the influential Australian biologist and anthropologist Baldwin Spencer was still promoting the 'science' of race. Spencer claimed that Aboriginal people had the mental capacity of children, with little control over their feelings, 'no sense of responsibility and, except in rare cases, no initiative'. (Nevertheless, Spencer praised their memory and care of children.) Spencer was soon to become president of the Victorian Football League (VFL), and it was footy that provided an opportunity for people like Doug Nicholls to prove Spencer wrong.

. . . . . .

'You should meet Pastor Douglas Nicholls, of Fitzroy, Melbourne, if you still think the Australian aboriginal is a simple Stone Age man incapable of taking any but the lowliest place in the technological society of the 20th century.' So began an *Australian Women's Weekly* profile in 1957 of one of the most amazing men to play Australian Rules football. It was a revealing start to a glowing portrait, a striking reminder of the attitudes that Nicholls had set his life against.

Doug Nicholls hadn't set out to change Australia, but help change Australia he did, though few people know of him these days. Born in 1906, he grew up in an Aboriginal reserve where his people were forced to live for their own 'protection', like many other Indigenous Australians of the time. In Nicholls's case it was the Cummeragunja Aboriginal Reserve on the New South Wales banks of the Murray River. The reserve was largely inhabited by members of the Yorta Yorta language group who had once lived along the Murray Valley but had been devastated by the arrival of the British. More than 80 per cent of the population had died in the first few decades after colonisation. It was a harsh environment and Nicholls had to endure the trauma of seeing his sixteen-year-old sister forcibly taken by police to a home which trained Aboriginal girls to work as domestic servants and prevented contact with family members. Nicholls's employment options were limited. He'd left school at eight to earn some money as a farmhand, but had little chance of advancement. Sport, however, provided a way out.

Growing up, Nicholls starred for the Cummeragunja footy team, which became a dominant force in the local league. Known as the 'Invincibles', the team won six premierships in eleven years through the 1920s and 1930s. Small even for those days at just over five feet (152 centimetres) tall, Nicholls was well built with pace to burn and soon graduated to the Goulburn Valley Football League, where he played for Tongala. Nicholls was celebrated as the 'Flying Abo', his electric play and high marking impressing crowds and his club alike – enough for them to find him a job. But the lure of the city was strong and soon a football talent scout convinced Nicholls to try his luck in Melbourne.

The year was 1927 and the 20-year-old Nicholls trained with the VFL club Carlton, but they cut him just before the season started. Nicholls wasn't surprised. The Carlton players had never seemed comfortable around him, with some complaining that he 'smelled'. It was Carlton's loss, as Nicholls demonstrated with four impressive years with the Victorian Football Association (VFA) side Northcote, helping them to a premiership, representing the VFA in interstate competition, and achieving renown as a 'brilliant wingman'.

Northcote helped Nicholls find a job with the local council, and he supplemented his income with other sporting feats, winning a number of prestigious running races. When Nicholls signed with Jimmy Sharman's legendary boxing troupe in 1931, the headline of the Melbourne *Herald* lamented, 'Doug Nicholls Lost to Football!' With Nicholls no longer at Northcote the VFL club Fitzroy pursued him, offering considerable payment and a job in the off-season as the curator of Fitzroy Oval. While Nicholls's experience with Carlton had made him wary of VFL sides, he was embraced by the Fitzroy team, with Haydn Bunton, the leading player in Victoria, going out of his way to make the 'prized recruit' feel welcome. Despite a lingering knee injury, Nicholls again starred, winning the Fitzroy best and fairest award in 1934, and becoming the first Aboriginal player selected for the VFL's representative Victorian team.

In a land always thirsty for more sports news, Doug Nicholls was a big story. Papers from around the country celebrated his sporting feats, noting how he made up for his lack of height with courage, speed and skill. Melburnians were especially fond of Nicholls, with a 1934 *Argus* newspaper profile declaring that it 'is safe to say that a more popular player never wore football boots in Australia'. It was an extraordinary statement, a testament to power of sport, to the way an athlete could capture the hearts and minds of a land mired in economic depression. But it also hints at the complexity of Australia's race relations. Comparisons with South Africa are often apt, but it is hard to imagine that country celebrating any black athlete during this period in such a way. Nicholls himself was well aware of the contradictions between the praise lavished on him and the appalling discrimination that other Indigenous Australians often faced. He knew he was a symbol of hope to members of the Yorta Yorta who followed his progress closely, and soon Nicholls was using his public profile to agitate on their behalf.

An active Christian since the early 1930s, Nicholls was also inspired by his great-uncle, William Cooper, who'd moved to Melbourne from Cummeragunja so he could receive a government pension. Back in 1887, Cooper had co-signed a letter to the Governor of Victoria requesting land rights, and he remained committed to the rights of Indigenous peoples. In 1935, Cooper helped found the Australian Aborigines' League, of which Doug Nicholls became an energetic member. One of the first acts of the league was to send a delegation to Canberra to lobby Commonwealth ministers for better rights. When this proved unsuccessful, the Victorian League joined with their New South Wales counterparts in the Aborigines Progressive Association. The result was a Day of Mourning held on Australia Day, 1938, protesting the 150th anniversary of colonisation.

Held in Sydney, the Day of Mourning was the first national action for Indigenous rights, with people sending in messages of support from around the country. Nicholls's eloquent appeal rang out among the assembled crowd:

> The public does not realise what our people have suffered
> for 150 years ... Put on reserves, with no proper education,
> how can Aborigines take their place as equals with whites?
> Now is our chance to have things altered. We must fight our
> very hardest in this cause. After 150 years our people are still
> influenced and bossed by white people. I know that we could
> proudly hold our own with others if given the chance.

Sport had been like a 'university' for Doug Nicholls and now he began putting his education to work. After retiring from football in 1939, Nicholls became a Church of Christ minister, dedicating himself to the cause of Australia's Indigenous peoples, presiding over an Aboriginal congregation in Fitzroy, leading the Australian Aborigines' League and mentoring Aboriginal athletes. His aim was to 'raise all Aborigines throughout the Commonwealth to full Citizen Status and civil equality with whites in Australia'. Yet while sport had given Nicholls unprecedented opportunities and popularity, it was a barrier for others.

. . . . . .

'How "Australian" is this football game?' So asked Adelaide journalist Lawrie Jordan when he found out in 1953 that the Pingelly–Brookton Football Association had not only 'banned aboriginal football since 1948', but was seeking to make the ban permanent. 'It's a downright scandal', thundered the *Argus*'s Ken Moses when he found out about the ban and its proposed extension. Moses called on the Australian National Football Council to intervene if they wanted to 'use the title of "Australian" Rules for the code'. Faced with national pressure the Pingelly–Brookton Football Association relented, allowing clubs to have up to six 'natives' on their list, but only to play three in any one game. Yet just a year later the association was seeking clarification of just what 'native' meant. It was a question that pointed to the obsession that systems of racial segregation have with classifying race.

In essence, the issue was this: should people with one Aboriginal parent and one European parent be classified as Aboriginal or white? And the issue went beyond who could play football in a country association to matters of survival, hope and redemption. Australia's Indigenous peoples were supposed to be dying out, but what of those who were of supposedly mixed blood? It was a question that haunted the hamlet of Pingelly, and Australia's troubled race relations more generally.

Government policy around much of Australia was to treat so-called 'half-castes' as white in the hope of 'breeding out' their Aboriginality and therefore separating them from their 'doomed' Aboriginal heritage. It was an aggressive measure of supposed protection that can also be seen as an attempt to ensure the extinction of Indigenous peoples. But in places like Pingelly there was considerable resistance to such measures.

. . . . . .

In 1957 the Little Rock Central High School of Arkansas in the United States became the site of a famed battle over racial segregation. The Arkansas Governor defied the US Supreme Court by insisting that only white students could attend the school. In response, President Eisenhower brought in federal troops to ensure the safe enrolment of nine African American students. What is much less known in Australia is that in 1942 the white parents of Pingelly also insisted that their school remain segregated. Claiming that the 'half-caste' children were spreading diseases to their white schoolkids, parents withdrew around 200 children from the school, saying they would withhold them until the 'half-caste' children were taught in a separate classroom.

The strike drew attention to the appalling conditions on the Noongar reserve but also to the levels of continuing segregation in the town. The Pingelly Progress Association would later argue for better treatment of the 'natives', but the primary concern of the white parents was to ensure the separation of their children from the 'half-castes'.

When the Western Australian Government moved in 1954 to integrate Aboriginal people within the broader community, white residents of Pingelly once again resisted. The government was supplying funding for new houses for Noongar families, to be built near the centre of Wheatbelt towns like Pingelly and York. However, a deputation from the York Municipal Council and Pingelly Road Board asked the Minister for Housing to scrap the initiative because such a development would be 'detrimental' to both towns. Although the minister urged the deputation to consider Aboriginals 'as human beings, not animals', the plans eventually stalled.

. . . . . .

P ingelly was not an isolated example of segregation within Australia. In the early 1960s the eyes of Australia and much of the world were on the racial discrimination in South Africa and America's Deep South. Yet when a group of Sydney university students held a 'Freedom Ride' in 1965 modelled on US anti-segregation activists the 'Freedom Riders', they were confronted with intense racism. Led by another Indigenous sports star, soccer player Charles Perkins, their journey into western and coastal New South Wales exposed the discrimination faced by many Indigenous communities. It also showed their squalid living conditions on the outskirts of towns. In places such as Walgett, Moree, Kempsey and Bowraville, Aboriginal residents were often not served in shops and were systematically excluded from cafes, cinemas, clubs and swimming pools. The activists received a hostile reception. Their bus was twice run off the road by angry residents, and eggs and other projectiles were hurled at them. They responded by capturing much of this on film and tape. The distressing footage included comments by the vice-president of the Walgett Returned Services League that he would never allow an Aboriginal person to become a member. Never before had Australia's racial discrimination been so exposed. The ride featured on evening news bulletins and was also splashed across the front pages of newspapers.

The Freedom Ride was one example of the growing movement for the rights of Australia's Indigenous peoples. First Victoria, then New South Wales and South Australia removed their discriminatory laws. Then, in 1963, the Yolngu people of north-eastern Arnhem Land in the Northern Territory sent the federal government of Robert Menzies a bark petition asserting their land rights in response to the start of mining activities on their traditional lands. Three years later, Gurindji workers and their families walked off Wave Hill Station in the Northern Territory in protest against decades of appalling mistreatment while working for the British pastoral company Vesteys on land which had been theirs. All the while, Doug Nicholls and many others were working tirelessly to convince the Commonwealth Government of the need for a referendum to include recognition of Indigenous peoples in the constitution.

Menzies eventually agreed to hold a referendum in 1967. Yet with the referendum only weeks away, two magistrates in Pingelly went public with the claim that corporal punishment was the only effective way to discipline the local Indigenous people. 'No matter what all the do-gooders say in Perth', explained magistrate EO Lange, 'a whipping is the only form of punishment that Aborigines around here fear'. It was a disturbing sign that although the 'Yes' vote would be overwhelming, and sport provided a chance for Aboriginals like Lionel Rose and Doug Nicholls to be celebrated, shocking racist attitudes remained strong.

. . . . . .

The 1968 Summer Olympics in Mexico City were another powerful reminder of the ways in which sport and race could intersect. Australia's Peter Norman won the silver medal in the men's 200-metre race in a time that remains the fastest run by an Australian over that distance. But Norman is remembered much more for what occurred during the medal ceremony. The gold and bronze medals had been won by Tommie Smith and John Carlos respectively, both African Americans representing the United States. As the US national anthem played, Smith and Carlos bowed their heads and raised a fist, symbolising both their pride in their colour and their protest against the discrimination faced by people of colour in the USA. Ashamed by the racism underlying the White Australia Policy, Peter Norman supported the actions of Smith and Carlos by wearing an Olympic Project for Human Rights badge alongside the pair on the medal dais.

The image of the trio on the podium was stunning, and quickly became iconic. But all three athletes suffered as a result of their protest. Smith and Carlos were expelled from the Olympics, ostracised by US sporting officials and organisations, and subjected to hateful abuse and death threats. Norman's punishment was less public, but still had a major impact on his life. He was officially reprimanded by the Australian Olympic Committee, and felt shunned by the

Australian media. His non-selection for the 1972 Olympic Games also raised eyebrows. Decades later, Norman felt overlooked in the official ceremonies around the 2000 Sydney Olympics, and it was the USA Olympic team that invited him to join them and celebrated his role in the 1968 protest. It was a sign that actions against racism in Australia could still bring their own long-term burdens.

The decade in which Nicky Winmar, Gilbert McAdam, Wayne Ludbey and John Feder were born saw a groundswell of Aboriginal athletes compete at the highest level. In the 1960s, Australian Rules football players like Barry Cable, Syd Jackson, David 'Soapy' Kantilla, Percy Cummings and Graham 'Polly' Farmer made names for themselves in Perth, Adelaide and Melbourne. Aboriginal women also emerged, like tennis star Evonne Goolagong, cricketer Faith Thomas, and badminton champions, sisters Cheryl and Sandra Mullett.

But the frequent bouts of public affection lavished on Indigenous sporting stars did not mean Australia was free of racism. Indeed, these athletes would be tormented at times by racial abuse. Yet sport provided them with rare opportunities to excel and be celebrated for it. Doug Nicholls and Charles Perkins had taken these opportunities and then used them as a foundation for change. It was on their shoulders that Nicky Winmar and Gilbert McAdam would come to stand. But first they would find out about the harsh realities of racism in Australia. Wayne Ludbey and John

Feder would also be confronted by moments of racism when growing up, but their experiences were so different from those of Winmar and McAdam that they might have been living in another country.

2

Growing up in different Australias

'*I still can't believe it*'

Nicky Winmar stares at a turtle suspended in the park pond, the two lost in a shared stillness and silence for several minutes. The wind whistles through the trees in the empty Queens Gardens in Perth and rain clouds hang ominously low while we wait patiently to resume our conversation. We know Winmar is reluctant to talk about his 1993 protest, and the omens aren't good. He's given very few interviews on the subject over the past two decades, and we've read how he and his partner, Beth, regularly change phone numbers to elude the approaches of unwanted journalists. We are only here in this neutral zone of a deserted park through the intercession of mutual friends. But still, he's *invited* us here. The turtle twitches, and now Winmar is back, keenly responding to our questions as he warms to our interest in his life before *that* moment and the memories we help rekindle.

Two hours later we meet again at a pub to view the 2012 Melbourne Cup. As we gear up to watch Green Moon thunder to the finish line, Winmar warmly greets strangers who approach him to say hello. That day in Perth we see two sides of the former footballer: a kind, gracious and sometimes ebullient man who is at ease with us discussing his childhood and Noongar heritage; and a guarded, reticent, almost haunted antihero wary of being chased and defined by one incident so long ago. Yet he is happy we are writing this book, and very pleased to hear we've already yarned with his old St Kilda mate Gilbert McAdam around the kitchen table, chatted with photographer John Feder at a cafe in Sydney's Five Dock, and driven around Melbourne lanes with another lensman, Wayne Ludbey, talking and taking pictures of Winmar's gesture rendered in paint by graffiti artists.

Our day with Winmar convinced us beyond any doubt that this is an important story that needs to be told. Something in his spoken memories revealed the richness, depth and intricate forces underlying his 1993 on-field protest that mere accounts of the event cannot capture. The story did not begin or end on 17 April 1993. Our interviews with the four protagonists in the event – the two players and the two press photographers, all born within a few years of one another – helped lay bare the complex pathways that lead to and from Victoria Park that April day. And what struck us most when Winmar laughed as a beloved kangaroo dog leapt across his memories, or grimaced at reruns of school-day bullying, was the marked differences in the Australian childhoods of all four men and the impact of each on our understanding of Winmar's now iconic gesture.

. . . . . .

Neil Elvis 'Nicky' Winmar had been born on 25 September 1965 in Kellerberrin, but moved to nearby Pingelly as a young child with his parents Neal and Meryle, sister Heather and brothers Frank and Bevan. Like most others on the reserve, the Winmars lived in a small tin shack. Winmar remembers that there was no running water. The 'toilet facility was just a bucket' that had to be moved after use. The concrete floor just had a bit of lino on it. When it rained, 'we had to move the bed around' to stop it getting wet from gaps between the corrugated sheeting that made up the roof.

Segregated from the white townsfolk, the Noongar were still subject to abuse. Winmar remembers being racially taunted at school. It was like being bullied, and he hated it. Not surprisingly, perhaps, Winmar didn't enjoy his schooling. But he also made enduring friendships with some of the 'white fellas' he had classes with. 'We get on really well today when we see each other. We are good mates.'

Sport was his passion. Winmar tried his hand at everything. He was terrible at swimming, 'terrified of the cricket ball', but better at basketball, making it to grade A. Still, it was footy that he loved. Aussie Rules was a family and community obsession. Winmar's father Neal (who was also nicknamed Nicky), his grandfather Percy Winmar, and several cousins and uncles played locally. 'A lot of rellies were great players', reminisced Winmar, but many 'went for girlfriends instead of chasing footy. We grew up watching our uncles and relatives playing. We idolised our uncles and fathers.' Other Noongars from south-western Western Australia played at the highest level, including Barry Cable, Syd Jackson, Ted 'Square' Kilmurray and several sets of brothers like Maley, Eric and Bill Hayward, and later Dale and Derek Kickett, Jim and Phil Krakouer, and Keith and Phil Narkle. The Noongar player Stephen Michael – arguably the greatest Australian Rules footballer of all time – was beginning to dominate Western Australian football as Winmar started to dream of making a name for himself in the late 1970s.

The Winmar family frequently endured the bumpy ride to Perth to watch East Perth Royals, whose jerseys matched those of the local Pingelly team, and whose past heroes included Aboriginal players Polly Farmer, Kilmurray and Jackson. The advent of the ABC TV show 'The Winners' brought more expansive dreams for Winmar and his friends. Beginning in 1977, 'The Winners' aired each Sunday in the Aussie Rules states. It showed extended footage from the best VFL games played that Saturday, and also featured popular segments on the marks and goals of the round. The Winmar family would huddle round their black-and-white TV and take it in. 'We were all excited by it. It was great, you know, the old commentators back then. They were really fantastic.'

Every afternoon after school, Winmar and his mates would re-enact the scenes they'd witnessed on TV. An old salmon gum stump in a field at the back of their house was perfect for 'speccy' practice. One boy would stand on the smooth-barked stump, another would throw a football high in the air, and a third would launch himself to mark it, using the back of the boy on the stump as a stepladder. When it came to his turn, Winmar would imagine he was the St Kilda star Trevor Barker. 'I thought he was just fantastic when he took off and climbed over the pack. I wanted to do what he did.' Goalposts were also marked on the fence, while footy games were held alternately in three different backyards, each of which was named after a famous ground: one was the Melbourne Cricket Ground, another VFL Park (in Waverley, Melbourne), and the third was the main oval in Perth, Subiaco. Happy yells covered the occasional crashes when the ball spun through draughty windows into kitchens. Wet grounds were a feature of VFL footy, so Winmar and his friends would often water the MCG and VFL Park backyards so that they were similarly muddy and slippery.

Winmar's father worked on the local farms, shearing sheep among other tasks, but he wanted better things for his children, and pushed Nicky to train hard. 'He trained me and developed me and I just went out there and just worked hard in my training.' Nicky often travelled with his father when he went shearing. While his dad worked, the young Winmar spent the day tackling sheep and building the defensive skills he'd later be renowned for. Soon Nicky Winmar was excelling on the footy field. By the age of fifteen he was playing in Pingelly's senior team. The men he was now playing against didn't care that Winmar was young and very lightly built. 'They were rough as, they were. I have still got a sore jaw from those days', he recalled, rubbing his smooth-shaven face. Some of them also racially abused Winmar, but his dad told him to 'show them a clean pair of heels and just run'. The way Winmar tells it, spurred on by his father he 'just ran and got the footy' the best way he could. The records show that he was already a phenomenon, winning the 1980 Pingelly seniors best and fairest in his first season as a fifteen-year-old. Before long, scouts were travelling from Perth to see him play.

· · · · · ·

A young Gilbert McAdam was attracting the eyes of scouts at a similar time. Like Nicky Winmar, McAdam was an Indigenous Australian. But although he was born just eighteen months after Winmar, on 30 March 1967 in Alice Springs, McAdam's initial experiences of race and place were very different. In fact, McAdam doesn't remember experiencing any racism in Alice Springs. Instead, he was part of a family that became celebrated by the local community for its great sporting prowess.

The fourth child of Charlie and Val McAdam, Gilbert grew up wanting to emulate the feats of his older brother Greg. His four sisters – Margaret, Pamela, Elizabeth and Michelle – would play representative sport, as would his two younger brothers, Adrian and Ian. But it was Greg who first set the standard for Gilbert, playing for the Northern Territory in the Under 16s Schoolboys Carnival in 1976. A hard-working, highly skilled midfielder, Greg was selected in the All-Australian squad picked from the carnival. His performances also caught the eye of the North Adelaide Football Club, and in 1977 the club brought him to Adelaide. A year later, the sixteen-year-old Greg broke into the seniors and began his South Australian National Football League (SANFL) career. Over the next five years he would win the North Adelaide best and fairest twice and play for South Australia against Victoria in State of Origin football.

Like the Winmars and many others, the McAdam family loved watching 'The Winners'. North Melbourne won the flag in 1977, the first year the program was aired. Soon the McAdam family were barracking passionately for North. 'I used to love Malcolm Blight, a bloke called Keith Greig, and Ron Barassi. We loved Barass because Barass was the [North] coach. Mum and Dad loved him. We were all mad keen Kangaroos.' Yet it was Greg who was Gilbert's hero. 'I used to idolise my brother. There's no doubt about that, because he inspired me, see. Whatever he did I wanted to do. I wanted to be like him, but I wanted to be better than him.'

Soon Gilbert was showing that he was likely to be at least the sporting equal of his brother. As a ten-year-old, Gilbert played for the Northern Territory in Australian Rules football and captained the Territory's cricket and soccer teams. Together, he and his siblings filled their house with hundreds of sporting trophies. Their achievements pleased Charlie McAdam, though he didn't show his emotions in public. Instead the kids learnt of his pride from their mother. For many years Charlie McAdam also kept a deeper secret from his children – that he had been stolen from his mother as a child.

Charlie's father, James 'Jimmy' McAdam, was a Scottish pastoralist, the owner of Springvale Station near Halls Creek in the East Kimberley region of Western Australia. With his wife running a pub around over 100 kilometres away, Jimmy used his domestic cook, Kitty, for sex. One of the local dispossessed Kija people who lived on the station, Kitty gave birth to Charlie in the late 1930s. What she never told Charlie was that Jimmy McAdam initially wanted to kill him. Kitty fled Springvale with the man who became Charlie's stepfather, staying away from the station for about three months. The baby Charlie was oblivious to the drama around him, and his early memories of the station were largely positive ones – of days spent playing with his cousins and other Kija playmates, and of his Kija stepfather teaching him how to live off the land. But when he was about seven, Charlie was snatched from his mother by a Native Affairs officer. 'This bloke chased me and grabbed me. I was screaming and kicking and shouting, falling down on the ground and rolling around, and my mother was crying, trying to hang onto me.'

Charlie was one of the Stolen Generations, thousands of Indigenous children who were taken from their families and communities between 1909 and the 1970s. Theories and rationales abound as to why Australian governments committed these terrible acts. Did they really think it would protect the children and offer a better life? Or was it done to hasten the extinction of a race supposedly in inevitable decline? Though it was likely a combination of factors, the actions remain inexcusable. The notorious Moola Bulla reserve in the Kimberley that Charlie was first sent to treated the children they received with contempt. Charlie recalled the starving kids stealing food from the pigs, being flogged to the point that he could barely walk, and seeing someone chained, cuffed and electrocuted as punishment for misbehaviour. A few years later Charlie was taken to the Beagle Bay Mission, north of Broome, which was not as inhumane. Still, contact with family members was banned, with strict discipline and beatings routine.

When Charlie was finally able to leave as a young teenager, he returned to Springvale Station. The reunion with his mother remained the 'happiest day' of his life. 'We cried and cried, with joy I suppose. We had no contact over the years. They did not know if I was alive and I didn't know whether they were alive.' Charlie's trials were far from over – he was soon enduring harsh work as a very young teenage stockman – but he was out of the insidious institutions that haunted many.

After a number of jobs, including a short period boxing, Charlie married Val and settled down in Alice Springs. An Aranda woman, Val too had been stolen. Aged seven, she was sent down to Adelaide to live with a woman who was 'looking after' another half-dozen girls from Alice Springs and Adelaide. For eight years she had no contact with her family. When the woman she was lodged with died, the now fifteen-year-old Val was finally allowed to return home.

Even in communities like Alice Springs, there was something taboo about discussing the experiences of those who had been stolen. Gilbert McAdam remembers that there were whispers about who had been taken away and who hadn't. 'But it was all hush-hush. You weren't allowed to talk about it, but for some reason they just didn't speak about it because the governments used to tell them that it was a lie.' Charlie McAdam, however, was from Western Australia, so he was not one the community members knew about. For a long time he chose not to burden his children with the tales of his early life. Instead he taught them some bush skills – including taking the boys hunting kangaroos and teaching them how to prepare the meat – and together with Val instilled great discipline into them.

What Charlie didn't teach any of his children was his excellent horsemanship. When Gilbert later asked him why he hadn't, Charlie responded that 'it was a mug's game'. He said, 'Son, it was too hard'. Yet Gilbert feels that it was also because Charlie didn't want to have to revisit the 'many bad memories' he had from being a horseman. Like Neal Winmar, Nicky's dad, Charlie wanted something better for his kids. He was very happy, then, in 1981, when Gilbert left at the tender age of fourteen for Adelaide to further his sporting ambitions.

. . . . . .

John Feder also left home as a teenager in search of a better life. His family had journeyed to Australia from England in 1965 as 'Ten Pound Poms' when John was just three years of age. Fearing invasion from Asia, the Australian

Government had expanded its infamous White Australia Policy to include assisted migration from Europe and thus further populate Australia with people who could defend it if needed. Families and young adults from the British Commonwealth were particularly encouraged, only having to pay £10 for the boat trip to Australia as long as they then stayed for at least two years. Though Feder's mother was Irish and his father Italian, they had married in England and were able to join the hundreds of thousands who took advantage of the scheme.

Like many other Ten Pound Poms, Feder's family struggled to adapt to life in Australia. After arriving in Wollongong they settled in the northern suburb of Bulli. Home was a cramped miner's cottage. Feder's dad, Bruno, worked in the coalmines while his mum, Julia, cared for her three sons and one daughter, all the time pining desperately for her mother. John Feder's two brothers were much older than him and hated being in Wollongong. After a year, Julia was willing to endure the five-week boat trip to go back to England. She 'dragged' her family with her, but the two eldest sons stayed in Australia. One had a job, another was not far from getting one. Around two years later the family was back in Australia, this time for good.

It was not an unusual trajectory. About 25 per cent of the assisted British migrants returned home, with a further half of these then coming back to Australia. Yet it points to the difficulty of migrating to a strange land more than

15 000 kilometres from family and other support networks. John Feder certainly never felt like he fitted into life in Bulli. Despite the suburb having an Aboriginal name that referred to the two mountains in the area, Bulli was very white. It seemed turned in on itself, rather than interested in the rest of the world. Feder knew of only one other family with Mediterranean heritage. His sense of being out of place was furthered by an incident of racial abuse. 'I can always remember going to high school and this girl that I'd been in primary school with suddenly called me a wog one day and I was like, "What's that all about?" And then it dawned on me I guess. That was my first real touch of racism.'

It's likely that Feder's father also experienced racism. But if he did, he never spoke of it. He was a hard man who'd fought for Italy in the Second World War, then been captured and held as a prisoner of war in England. After the war he was allowed to remain in England, and he met his wife while working on a farm. She herself was a migrant, her family of twelve kids having moved from Ireland to England when her father died after the First World War. The pairing of John Feder's parents was not a usual one, and Bulli was not a town that nurtured or supported the unusual. Although Feder didn't recall other incidents of racism, he felt vulnerable about his father's heritage. 'I must admit I used to lie about Dad's heritage and stuff like that to some of my friends at school. Looking back I can't believe it.'

Bulli didn't feel like it offered much of a future, at least for the young Feder. Most of his classmates ended up in the steelworks or the mines. Yet like Gilbert McAdam, John Feder was blessed with an older brother who inspired him to strive for something greater. Ten years older than John, Tony Feder had got a press job at the *Illawara Mercury* in 1967 and developed an interest in photography. He later moved to Melbourne, where he found a job as a sports photographer at the *Age*. In the early 1970s Tony Feder visited Bulli, bringing with him a camera for John that he taught him how to use. From that moment on, John Feder was forever taking pictures. He'd take pictures of his nephew, of the nearby trots (harness racing), of cars coming down the Princes Highway that bordered their house, and of anything related to sport, 'because I always loved sport'. Then he'd go into the wardrobe to methodically develop his pictures, transferring the images from film to paper by way of a small tank, chemicals, and the judicious use of light. It was a basic small-scale operation that would become increasingly sophisticated as Feder acquired more equipment.

When Feder was holidaying in Melbourne as a young teenager, his brother Tony took him along to a golf tournament he was shooting. John of course brought his camera. One of John's shots of Rodger Davis was so good that Tony submitted it to his newspaper, the *Age*. It earned John his first front page (though the by-line was Tony's). Compared to Bulli, Melbourne seemed to John to be free, vibrant and exciting. A couple of years later, aged sixteen, he moved to Melbourne to stay with his brother while he completed his final two school years at Banyule High. In contrast to Wollongong, John 'fitted in straightaway'. An immediate love affair with Australian Rules football assisted his passage.

The first football match John Feder attended was the Carlton–Collingwood grand final in 1979. From the start he found the atmosphere 'intoxicating'. A close friend took him to the game. 'He was a Carlton supporter, and just seeing how involved he was, I'd never seen anything like it in my life.' The fierce tribalism of the crowd was compelling, 'the two sides going at it'. And the game was amazing. Collingwood dominated early, keeping Carlton goalless for most of the first half. Yet the Blues finished the half with five quick goals to somehow take the lead. Now it was Carlton's turn to dominate, before Collingwood kicked three straight goals to be within a kick with just a few minutes remaining. Then came a passage of play that would enter the folklore of the game. Carlton's Wayne Harmes kicked the ball into a forward pocket, chased his own kick, then dived full-length to hit the ball back into play as it was rolling over the boundary line. The footy ended in the arms of a team-mate who kicked the sealing goal. All the while Collingwood barrackers howled in rage that the ball had already been out of play.

The Grand Final was talked about all through the summer that followed. John Feder was hooked. Now footy and photography were passions. He studied photography at school and went to the football every Saturday with his best friend. John followed North Melbourne, his mate went for Carlton, so they alternated the games they saw. When he finished school in 1981, Feder hoped to pursue a career that would bring together photography and footy.

. . . . . .

Around the same time, Wayne Ludbey was beginning to nurture similar dreams. Like John Feder, Ludbey had a parent of Italian heritage, in this case his mother. Ludbey also shared a familial connection to the world of newspapers. His father, Don, co-owned the *Cairns Post*. In the mid-1960s Don sold the paper to the Herald and Weekly Times and took to working for them instead. When Wayne was only a few years old, the family moved to Port Moresby, where his father trained Papua New Guineans to run and manage every facet of the local *Post-Courier*. It was an idyllic six years for Wayne. He attended a military school where kids from all over the world mingled happily together. 'My best friend was a Papuan guy and there were Chinese, Dutch, German, English and Australian.' The 'friendly environment' made it seem like 'multiculturalism was a natural thing'.

In the early 1970s, Don Ludbey was appointed manager of a new Herald and Weekly Times printing plant in

Port Melbourne. The shock of moving to Melbourne was intense. While Feder had felt blessed to be able to live in Melbourne and fitted straight in, the reverse was true for Wayne Ludbey. Not only was the weather cold and miserable, the kids at the primary school Wayne attended in East Malvern were also less than friendly. It was 'a very nasty schoolyard ... very competitive and very nasty'. In his first few weeks Ludbey heard someone being called a 'wog' for the first time. 'I remember saying to someone, "What does that mean? What does wog mean?"' When the answer came, Ludbey 'felt sick'. Although Ludbey's racial awakening came as something new and shocking to him, his mother, Mary, who had shielded her toddler son from the racism levelled against his Italian relatives in Cairns, remains pleased that 'he didn't know the half of it'.

Wayne hated the primary school. High school in Glen Waverley was more of the same, and he hated that as well. But, as with Nicky Winmar, sport, and in particular Australian Rules football, was a solace. 'I started playing footy for the Glen Waverley Hawks and loved it.' Ludbey showed talent for the game and began to move through the ranks. He also moved schools, taking his final two years at Kingswood College in Box Hill. It was an unusual Methodist-run school that modelled itself more on a university than on traditional schools, and students were treated like adults. There were 'no uniforms, no bells' and the 'teachers were great'. Ludbey blossomed, revelling in the art class which allowed him to start developing photography skills. He also relished the history lessons.

The history teacher, Richard Cotter, enjoyed the way the relaxed Kingswood style suited and often inspired students who had fallen through the cracks at other schools. In 1981, when Ludbey was in his final year, the Australian historian Henry Reynolds published *The Other Side of the Frontier*. It was the first major study of the ways Indigenous Australians, like Yagan the Noongar warrior, had resisted and fought against the invasion of their lands by Europeans. Previous Australian histories had largely focused on the experiences of the colonisers. Reynolds was at the forefront of an initially small group of historians seeking to understand how colonisation affected the traditional landowners. He uncovered tales of resistance, war and atrocity. The taking of Australia had not been the peaceful settlement the British had spoken of. Reading the book shortly after it came out, Cotter was 'stunned' and 'astonished'. 'It hit me over the head.'

Cotter felt 'it was the sort of thing that Australians should know about'. He immediately began teaching about the frontier wars sparked by the invasion of Australia. Wayne Ludbey was one of many of Cotter's students to be fascinated by these tales. For the first time 'we learned about the black resistance ... to the colonisation of Australia ... it's one of the few subjects I actually did well in'. Yet, like many other Australians, including Feder, Ludbey was unaware of the current discrimination faced by Australia's Indigenous peoples and their resistance to this.

Although they grew up with strikingly different experiences of Australia, Winmar, McAdam, Feder and Ludbey all entered the 1980s still delighting in the joys found in Australian Rules football. Ludbey was competing alongside future VFL players Silvio Foschini and Brad Gotch – and doing well. Then he broke his arm in a game. Later he heard that there was a scout at the game who, on seeing Ludbey injured, put a line through his name. The path Winmar and McAdam would take of playing footy for a living would not be available to him. Instead, like Feder, he would find another way of crafting a career around football. All four, however, would have moments in the 1980s where the racism associated with the game shocked them.

. . . . . .

In 1968, the same year as the 'Black Power Salute', the Australian anthropologist WEH Stanner had lamented the 'Great Australian Silence'. A 'cult of forgetfulness' or 'disremembering' was 'practised on a national scale' with regard to the history of Australia's Indigenous peoples. This silence had been punctured by key events like the 1967 referendum and the moment in 1975 when prime minister Gough Whitlam handed back land to Vincent Lingiari and his Gurindji people, but then it would return. And it shaped the journeys of Nicky Winmar, Gilbert McAdam, Wayne Ludbey and John Feder.

Winmar grew up in an environment that was racist, but where racism could not be combated openly. Instead, he was taught to run faster than those who wished to torment him. McAdam grew up in a place that seemed free of racism, yet his family and community were marked by the impact of the Stolen Generations, an impact that could only be spoken about in whispers, if at all. Both Wayne Ludbey and John Feder had encountered aspects of racism in different parts of Australia, but both were ignorant of the contemporary struggle of Indigenous Australians for justice. Both were enveloped by the silence. Wayne Ludbey, at least, was fortunate enough to be taught of the frontier resistance, of struggles that shaped Australia but were written out of history by the victorious British. Feder had been taught nothing of the history of Indigenous Australians. 'I still can't believe it', he noted recently, adding that it was 'a disgrace' that he hadn't been taught any of this at school. 'This is their country, basically, and we really knew nothing about them.'

3

Formative moments

'I felt nauseous'

London 1988. A holidaying Wayne Ludbey was enjoying a dip at a public baths. He was overseas for the first time since leaving Port Moresby as a child, and enjoying his first extended break since starting as a press photographer in 1982. The last thing he expected was for the dark shadow of Australia's racism to follow him to the other end of the world. But that is exactly what it did, in the form of a large and dreadlocked West Indian whose initial friendliness cooled when he discovered where Wayne was from. That chill soon became a full-blown harangue. 'He took me to the cleaners about racism in Australia', Ludbey recalled years later. At the time, though, Ludbey thought, 'Steady on!', but his accuser was so familiar with the chapter and verse of

Australia's shame that the sheer force of the poolside assault inspired only a cowed silence. It was the kind of incident that he would never forget, one that altered his perspective and, in its memorable way, focused the lensman's eye that would frame and capture Winmar's spontaneous protest at Victoria Park.

Ludbey's innocent ignorance typified the attitude that prevailed in the 1980s, when Indigenous Australians were gaining increasing prominence, especially in the arts and sport, and it was still possible to hold the delusion that race relations in Australia were nothing worth worrying about. The signing in 1982 of high-profile WAFL brothers Jim and Phil Krakouer by North Melbourne, and Maurice Rioli by Richmond, signalled a new wave of Indigenous players coming to play footy in Melbourne. The Aboriginal land rights movement also continued to grow. And yet, as Nicky Winmar, Gilbert McAdam, Wayne Ludbey and John Feder immersed themselves in footy, Australia's political leaders began to build towards a celebration of 200 years of colonisation without any meaningful acknowledgment of the suffering that colonisation had inflicted on the traditional owners of the land. Instead, as Ludbey had been made painfully aware, it was often people outside Australia who knew more about the discrimination and injustices faced by Indigenous Australians.

. . . . . .

Sport and politics have long been entangled, but their intimate connections are not always obvious. In the twentieth century, however, major sporting contests often showcased and enacted political agendas. Think of Hitler's celebration of Nazism at the 1936 Berlin Olympics, the 1972 massacre of Israeli athletes in Munich, and the US-led boycott of the 1980 Moscow Olympics. In 1982, as Winmar, McAdam, Ludbey and Feder began their careers, Indigenous activists sought to use the Brisbane Commonwealth Games to highlight, protest and transform Queensland's inequitable land rights legislation. In so doing, they were following in the recent footsteps of anti-racism activists who had begun using major sporting events to expose racist politics.

In the aftermath of the Black Power salute at the 1968 Mexico City Olympics, anti-apartheid activists began targeting sport as a way to draw attention to South Africa's appalling treatment of those whose skin colour was other than white. South Africa had been ousted from the Olympics in 1964. Now campaigners wanted to ban them from major international sporting contests. In Australia this big push began in 1971 when anti-apartheid protestors disrupted a tour by the South African surf lifesaving team. Only a few months later, opposition to a tour by South Africa's rugby union team, the Springboks, gained the support of trade unions and some Australian players. The protests drew mass international as well as national attention, highlighting police brutality against protesters as well as the issues at stake. The Queensland Government declared a state of emergency for one month to suppress the wave of demonstrations. Down south in Melbourne some 5000 protesters laid siege to Olympic Park, with charges by mounted police, crashing truncheons and broken heads turning the banks of the Yarra into a virtual war zone.

Attention then turned to the forthcoming 1971–72 tour of Australia by the South African cricket team. Don Bradman – still Chairman of the Australian Cricket Board – was inclined to let the tour continue because he believed the white South African cricketers personally opposed apartheid. Nonetheless, he travelled to South Africa to speak with prime minister John Vorster, a notorious supporter of Hitler and the Nazis during the war years. Vorster told Bradman that black people did not have the intelligence to deal with the intricacies of cricket. Bradman is said to have replied, 'Have you ever heard of Gary Sobers?' Yet Bradman was reluctant to cancel the tour, only doing so after advice from the federal Liberal government left him in no doubt that the visit would never be allowed to proceed. The South African team was replaced with a multi-racial touring party led by Gary Sobers and including several South African test players. Nonetheless, Bradman continued to push for future South African tours.

Anti-apartheid campaigners continued to target sporting events. The 1973 Springboks tour of New Zealand was postponed. Then, after the New Zealand All Blacks toured South Africa in 1976, the first sporting boycotts occurred around the issue of race. Twenty-eight African and Arab nations withdrew from the 1976 Montreal Olympics in protest at the New Zealand tour, while China cancelled a badminton tour of New Zealand. A year later, the members of the British Commonwealth adopted the Gleneagles Agreement to support the campaign against apartheid and discourage sporting competition with South Africa. When New Zealand defied this in 1981 by allowing a Springboks tour, the country faced the greatest acts of civil disobedience in its history. Soon after, New Zealand was notified that any further South African tours would lead to its suspension from the Commonwealth Games.

. . . . . .

The stunning success of the anti-apartheid sporting campaigns did not translate easily to the Australian struggle for Indigenous rights. Indeed, as historian Jennifer Clark noted, Australian reformers 'were more interested in the 1960s and early 1970s in the campaign against apartheid than in improving conditions for Aborigines'. When the Aborigines Advancement League in Victoria wrote to the Victorian anti-apartheid co-ordinator in 1971, they were told it would be hard to sustain a campaign without having a sports event to oppose. The 1982 Commonwealth Games provided just such an opportunity and Indigenous activists seized the moment without reservation. The Queensland Government had set itself against the land rights movement, abolishing the Aurukun and Mornington Island reserves and sacking the legally elected Aboriginal Council in Aurukun. Aboriginal activists initially proposed an international boycott of the Games, hoping African countries in particular would endorse opposition to both the state government's attempts to stymie land rights and Canberra's subdued response to these actions. When the boycott momentum waned, organisers instead planned protests to capitalise on the mass media presence during the games.

The Queensland Government responded by passing the *Commonwealth Games Act 1982*, which banned unauthorised protests, and classified pamphlets, badges, flags and placards as illegal weapons. It gave police the power to detain people for 48 hours on suspicion that the person was about to commit an offence, and allowed police to search homes without a warrant. In addition, there was no right to challenge the behaviour of police in court. Despite these draconian restrictions, a series of marches and other actions did occur. In one bold action, fourteen protesters smuggled Aboriginal flags and banners into the stadium and unfurled them during the highly anticipated final of the women's 400-metres sprint starring Australian medal favourite Raelene Boyle. These actions disrupted the Games only minimally, but they did attract the attention of the international media to Aboriginal land and human rights issues. As sports scholar Naomi Shannon noted, the games had 'reignited hidden, yet never dormant or idle Aboriginal pride and fortitude that carried on into the 1990s and through to the present'.

For Australian poet Bruce Dawe, the Brisbane protesters were competitors 'for the lonelier gold that comes later, the red and black of history'. Future competitors were being shaped on the footy ovals around Australia in the same period. Nicky Winmar was one. In 1982 the sixteen-year-old was outgrowing Pingelly and setting his sights on broader horizons. Just as he had recreated the muddy Victorian footy fields in his backyard as a boy, as a young man he looked to Victoria for his football idols, VFL players like North Melbourne's Malcolm Blight and St Kilda's Trevor Barker. Closer to home, he revered Benny Vigona, an Indigenous player from the Northern Territory who from the late 1970s played nearly 200 games for South Fremantle, the WAFL club that would sign Winmar in 1982.

. . . . . .

The South Fremantle Bulldogs were actively recruiting in 1982 following the retirement of several players and the loss of star player Maurice Rioli to Richmond in the VFL. Mick Moylan, the club's football development officer, spent the year scouring the club's country zones, identifying over 30 young men who were invited to train or play within the club's senior club structure – the Colts and Reserves. Winmar was among the chosen few. Playing for Pingelly in the ten-team Upper Great Southern League – in the centre of South's rural fan and player base – Winmar had made his mark in the Wesfarmers Country Week carnival at sixteen and in other Colts competition that year.

Winmar's speed and ball-handling skills particularly impressed Bulldogs players and officials who went to Pingelly to watch a game. 'Spellbound' by Winmar, South Fremantle coach Mal Brown cancelled the rest of his plans and instead met with Winmar and his family. A charismatic and controversial footy figure, Brown had played for and then coached East Perth, Claremont and South Fremantle in the WAFL, and had also played briefly with Richmond in the VFL. Brown had also recruited the Krakouers to the WAFL, and had previously coached a number of other outstanding Western Australian Aboriginal footballers including Maurice Rioli, Stephen Michael, Basil Campbell, Willy Roe and Benny Vigona. Winmar recalls sitting on his uncle's veranda with his parents as they discussed his future with Brown while the big kangaroo dog ran about.

In late 1982, Winmar had moved to Perth to participate in South Fremantle's 1983 pre-season program. He was the only player from Pingelly and one of only a few kids from regional Western Australia among the dozen or so new recruits. 'I was surprised when I was asked up here – it's a big thing, for country boys', Winmar later said. Other new recruits included Cyril Rioli (Senior) from Darwin. Winmar now laughs at his idea of pre-season – in Pingelly it meant turning up a week before footy started, whereas in Perth he was kept busy for six to eight weeks. The training paid off, with Winmar in fine form during the pre-season. Excited commentators compared his movements and ability to Phil and Jim Krakouer, the former Claremont players who were already starring for North Melbourne.

Like the Krakouer brothers, Winmar initially struggled with the fierce racism he experienced in the WAFL. 'There was a lot of racism back in those days', he told us. If he retaliated by 'smacking someone in the mouth' then he'd get suspended. 'They'd say it's not on that you hit somebody. But it wasn't on when you'd call us a racist name. Why can't you do something about that? Nothing was done.' Winmar found out about how the system worked in his first match. Starting the season in the Reserves, he was immediately reported and suspended for two weeks. As punishment, the Bulldogs relegated him back to the Colts and to a new climb back up the ranks.

Racist abuse such as that experienced by the rookie Winmar had long been a part of Australian sport. Evonne Goolagong recalled being called a 'nigger' by a fellow Australian player in Sydney in 1967. The masterful Ella brothers received 'torrents' of abuse while playing rugby union through the 1970s and 1980s. When Mark and Glen

Ella were chosen to play for Australia against Scotland in 1982 ahead of Queensland pair Roger Gould and Paul McLean, the Brisbane crowd 'booed and abused their every move'. It felt like playing in South Africa, noted Mark Ella later. Cricket was not immune either. Although Australia had feted the West Indies cricket team in 1960–61 and had refused to play cricket against South Africa since 1971, both the Australian crowds and senior cricketers racially abused members of the West Indies team in 1975–76. 'Go back to the trees, black bastards', chanted sections of the crowd in between urging the Australian fast bowlers to 'Kill, Kill, Kill!' Battered by the abuse, along with the aggressive pace of Dennis Lillee and Jeff Thomson, West Indies captain Clive Lloyd moulded an uncompromising team based on a terrifying pace attack of their own that played for black pride. In the lead-up to the England v West Indies in 1976, the South African–born captain of England, Tony Greig, announced that they planned to make the West Indians 'grovel'. The incensed West Indies team made Greig grovel instead, smashing the English 3–0. They would not lose another test series for fifteen years.

Leading Indigenous Australian Rules football players faced constant abuse. Syd Jackson, another Noongar man, played footy at the elite level for thirteen years, first with East Perth and then with Carlton. 'For myself and any other Aborigine who has played football at the top level, racist abuse remains a constant. You expect it every Saturday, if not from the opposition players, then from the spectators either as you walk onto the ground or as you are leaving.'

As he, too, sought to establish himself at the elite level, Winmar yearned to make a statement against the abuse. But he was a sixteen-year-old living by himself in a new city – 'I found it hard living there by myself'. Winmar also had to juggle several new responsibilities. He worked part-time handling scallops in a West Perth fish shop in his rookie year. Later he worked for the East Fremantle Town Council and enrolled at Fremantle Technical College. The constant racism made his life even harder. Club officials would occasionally talk with Aboriginal players about it, but mostly they 'told you to go out and play footy'. Winmar recalls that a lot of the young Indigenous players would go back home 'because they felt unsafe being in Perth'. Adelaide was similar to Perth in that respect. In the 1950s a young Charles Perkins experienced almost constant racial abuse and discrimination in Adelaide, finding an escape only in the marginal world of soccer and its migrant communities.

. . . . .

As Gilbert McAdam would discover, not so much had changed by 1982. The fourteen-year-old moved from Alice Springs to Adelaide to play in the Under 17s at the invitation of the North Adelaide footy club. The club paid for his schooling – at Nailsworth Tech on Regency Road –

as it had done for his older brother Greg a few years earlier. Greg McAdam had experienced racism for the first time in Adelaide. Lighter skinned than Gilbert, he initially found it 'really funny'. The 'people who were trying to put me down with racist comments couldn't identify what nationality I was because I had light skin and an Afro hairstyle. People didn't know whether to call me wog or black'. But Greg was appalled when his family came down to see him play and were abused in his company. '"You're OK but he's not OK" was the attitude. How can people say that when the other person next to me could be my first cousin or my uncle or someone?'

With his darker skin, Gilbert was immediately confronted with racist acts and abuse. 'I experienced it straightaway at school. Bang. First two days. Straightaway. Then, because I was playing Under 17s, I got it on the footy field straightaway. Then I got it in shops and wherever. I felt it all the time.' Curiously, nobody had forewarned him of racism – he thinks his parents wanted him to work it out for himself. But McAdam was resilient. 'I was a pretty strong person before I got there because of Mum and Dad, so whatever came my way I was pretty resilient and pretty strong and pretty proud of who I was.' He also credits other factors for his ability to handle the racism served out in those days. His Under 17s coach helped him understand the on-field slurs were tactical, aimed to upset him and put him off his game. "He used to say, "No, don't worry about them.".' McAdam lived with a non-Aboriginal family, who reinforced that message. The combined advice struck a chord. 'I think I got taught to be a team player at such a young age that by the time I got there I was already strong enough to cope with it as long as I had those people in my circle to reinforce this and reinforce that.'

One of the people in Gilbert's circle was his uncle, Elliot McAdam. The younger brother of Charlie, Elliot was born in 1951 after Jimmy McAdam married Dorcas Wesley, who had also been stolen from her family due to her classification as a 'half-caste'. After his parents died, Elliot was prevented from contacting the Aboriginal side of his family, and eventually ran away to reunite with his family in Darwin. In the late 1960s, Elliot lived with Charlie and Val for a year. Later he moved to Adelaide where he dedicated himself to working for Aboriginal rights. Greg lived with his uncle Elliot, who drove him to and from footy training. While Gilbert chose to live with a Catholic family rather than his uncle, Elliot took an active interest in his life and career. He was a great supporter who was as inspired by Gilbert's work ethic as by his all-round sporting talent. 'He was always independent and dedicated. Gilbert could have played soccer for Australia if he had wanted to – he was good enough. I also think that Gilbert could have played at least Sheffield Shield cricket; in fact, all the boys could have, had they wanted to. Gilbert was an outstanding cricketer. He used to score centuries in Adelaide all the time.'

Gilbert McAdam's school also played a supportive role, quickly making him house captain of athletics, cricket and footy. A couple of schoolyard fights over racial taunts remain strong in his memory, but he is now good mates with some of his old tormentors. Being in Adelaide also enabled him to follow Greg's career. Gilbert remembers sitting proudly in the stands watching Greg play State of Origin for South Australia, which at that time was hugely popular. When North Adelaide stymied Greg's first opportunity to join the VFL, the perceived injustice threatened to derail Gilbert's own career. When he finished school, Gilbert refused North Adelaide's offer to play and instead returned to the Northern Territory. At the time he said he was homesick, but in truth he didn't want to play for the team that had mistreated his brother.

. . . . . .

B ack over in Perth, Winmar also drew on family connections to deal with the hurt of racist abuse. He missed his parents deeply, but persevered, proving himself in the Colts and then the Reserves. 'Up … down … and back up again' was how WAFL's match-day program, the *Football Budget*, referred in 1983 to the way Winmar climbed back after his early suspension. When injuries and a case of shingles wiped out South Fremantle's regular centreline in late May, Winmar's toil was rewarded. On Saturday 28 May

1983, he debuted in the senior team against West Perth. Now he did not disappoint, scoring one goal and leaving 'no doubt about his class with a solid first-up performance'. A week later Winmar confirmed his ability in a 'brilliant burst', kicking three goals in the final quarter and being named one of three 'Best Players' by the *West Australian*. Winmar, they confidently claimed, 'is a player of the future'.

From playing only thirteen of 23 games in the 1983 season because of his late start, Winmar established himself as a top performer for the Bulldogs in 1984. Observers described the 180-centimetre, 69-kilogram wearer of the Bulldogs' number 34 jersey as a 'brilliant young utility player' and 'one of the exciting youngsters in the WAFL'. The *Football Budget* typified the exuberance about his ability in his second season: 'Aged just 18, Winmar seems to be able to do the impossible, to go where angels fear to tread … and yet come out with the ball and dispose of it with apparent ease'.

Despite his 'undoubted brilliance', Winmar struggled when Don Haddow replaced Mal Brown as coach in 1985. Winmar briefly resigned from the Bulldogs early that season, and in 1986 again returned to Pingelly a couple of times. Two other Aboriginal players, Benny Vigona and Willie Roe, also briefly left the team in 1986. Winmar's 1986 season was so truncated that he only played twelve games. Football commentators began to write of his 'bursts of inconsistency'. Despite this, his skills on the ground continued to wow spectators. Journalists still praised Winmar but questioned his focus. The *West Australian* described him as one of the 'most talented players when he concentrates on playing the game'. Even to Haddow, he was 'simply too good a player' to let go. By the time Winmar was 20 years old, clubs from the VFL were circling, attracted by his magical skills but concerned by his inconsistency.

Winmar's break came in late 1986 on the eve of the VFL's expansion into Western Australia and Queensland. Hawthorn had just defeated Carlton in the grand final. Essendon, the winner of the previous two premierships, were keen on Winmar and organised a meeting with their coach, Kevin Sheedy. The embryonic West Coast Eagles also showed interest. Nicky was particularly attracted to playing for the Eagles because it would have allowed him to stay in Western Australia, close to his family and friends. But both teams were beaten to the punch by St Kilda.

Former Saints official and player Stuart Trott had thought 'his eyes were deceiving him' when he watched a 'teenage Winmar decimate Swan Districts' and provided a glowing report. Although St Kilda had been blessed with some brilliant individuals like Trevor Barker and Tony Lockett, they'd struggled for playing depth, languishing around the bottom of the ladder since their last finals appearance in 1973. Excited by Trott's report, St Kilda was determined to attract Winmar across to Melbourne as part of its strategy to lift the club out of its doldrums. In 1986 it enlisted the help of John King, a former country footballer who helped recruit and advise Aboriginal players. King and Winmar had met around 1983 when Winmar had travelled to Victoria to play in an Aboriginal All-Stars match in Shepparton that King had helped organise.

At the time, Victorian clubs could recruit players from interstate by signing them to what was termed a 'form four' contract. King flew to Perth in late 1986. His mission was to bring Winmar back to Melbourne so that he could sign the form four with the Saints. Fearing that the Eagles might get wind of this and make a pre-emptive offer, King adopted the tactics of Cold War agents to keep his discussions with Winmar secret. For three days they moved between hotels, with Winmar ordering room service for every meal and avoiding the phone. In order to maintain the subterfuge, King booked late-night airfares for the pair under the names 'Mr and Mrs King'. 'It was like going from Russia to America', Winmar recalled. They were so successful that not even Winmar's parents knew until he rang them from Melbourne to break the news. They 'didn't know what to say'. Everyone was 'just so shocked at the time'.

For St Kilda, the signing of Nicky Winmar was a 'coup' to be celebrated. Tempering the elation, with his eye on the job ahead, Murray Abblitt, the Saints' manager, acknowledged Winmar's reputation as well as his ability. 'Everybody we spoke to in Perth told us Nicky could play ... They told us he was a better player than Phil Narkle. They also told us he was inconsistent, unreliable and would be hard to handle. We took him on that basis and we aren't trying to change him. He's been told what's expected of a senior player and now it's up to him.'

In many ways being in Melbourne was even harder for Winmar than being in Perth. Winmar's family was even further away now and the weather was worse. 'At first I didn't know what I was doing. I went to Melbourne and I said, "Oh no! How big is this place?" It was a big move.' John King was a crucial supporter. Winmar worked with him over the course of his first pre-season. Winmar pounded the streets of inner-city Carlton and Brunswick every morning at 6 am, with King following in a car, 'tooting the horn every time he slackened the pace'. The incoming St Kilda coach Darrel Baldock was another supporter. The captain of St Kilda's only premiership-winning team in 1966, Baldock 'was a good bloke' who 'gave me a lot of confidence'. On the back of his strong pre-season, Winmar was selected for the opening game of the 1987 season against Geelong at the Saints' home ground, Moorabbin Oval. St Kilda had finished last in each of the previous four years, but started brightly, building to a 33-point lead at half-time only to fade to a painful 1-point loss. Winmar was one of the positives, picking up 17 possessions and kicking a goal in his VFL debut.

It was the start of an impressive season. Winmar played 20 of 22 games, kicked 37 goals and came second in the club's best and fairest voting. Tony Lockett was a key beneficiary.

Time after time Winmar delivered precise kicks to the burly full-forward, who kicked 117 goals. Lockett not only won the Saints' best and fairest, but he shared the VFL's highest individual honour – the Brownlow Medal, awarded to the fairest and best player as adjudged by the umpires – with Hawthorn's John Platten. The pair had 20 votes apiece, while Winmar received a more than creditable 10 votes. The Saints had struggled for much of the year, but won six of their last eight games to finish tenth with hope for the future.

Racist abuse was still an ugly part of Victorian football, though it had been worse in Perth. Still, it was one of the things that stopped Winmar feeling comfortable in Melbourne. 'It took a long time' to feel more at ease – 'about two or three years'. Often Winmar wanted to go back to Pingelly, but St Kilda weren't going to let him go easily. 'I tried a couple of times to come home but they followed me and wanted me to come back.' Yet if life off the field was hard, Winmar continued to excel on the field. The 1988 season saw further improvement on an individual level, though the Saints regressed. With established stars like Tony Lockett and Trevor Barker unavailable for most of the season, the team slipped back to last place. With first-year player Robert Harvey, Winmar was a shining light. He kicked a club-high 43 goals from 21 games, and again came second in the club best and fairest, this time to Danny Frawley.

. . . . . .

That same year, Gilbert McAdam began his professional football career in Adelaide. On occasion from 1985
to 1987, he had played with the Waratahs in the Northern
Territory Football League. He was part of the Territorian
teams that defeated Essendon and the Sydney Swans in the
annual Australia Day games staged by the NTFL in January 1986 and 1987. His performances in the Under 18s Teal
Cup in 1984 and early Darwin games with the Waratahs
led the WAFL team Claremont to recruit him for the 1986
season. But he wasn't sure he wanted to play footy for a living. McAdam was also gripped with homesickness in Perth.
Four games into the season he made a sudden decision to
leave Perth, and 'jumped on the bus, took off back to Darwin and came back to Alice Springs'. He sat out most of
1987 season, but then a change in his personal circumstances led him to give footy another 'crack'. McAdam was newly
married and now a child was on the way. 'I thought, "No,
it's not about us anymore, it's about our kids now".'

Signed up by Central District in the SANFL in 1988,
McAdam 'killed them' in his first year. He credits his coach,
Neil 'Knuckles' Kerley, with giving him 'that much confidence that I believed that I could do anything. He hard-
ly ever said anything to me. He just let me play the way I
wanted to play'. McAdam reciprocated Kerley's faith. 'He
was prepared to meet me 50:50, so I thought "Yeah, I'm

going to give him blood, sweat and tears, this bloke. If he's prepared to give me that opportunity, I'm going to give him my blood, my sweat, my tears".' The result was one of the most impressive debut seasons those in Adelaide had ever seen. Gilbert McAdam played so well that he was runner-up to Sturt's Greg Whittlesea for the coveted Magarey Medal, awarded annually to the player voted the 'fairest and most brilliant player' in the SANFL.

. . . . . .

At the same time that Nicky Winmar and Gilbert McAdam were beginning to wow crowds in Melbourne and Adelaide, much of Australia was celebrating. The year 1988 marked the bicentennial of the arrival of Captain Arthur Phillip and the convict First Fleet at Sydney Cove on 26 January 1788. Official celebrations included the arrival of the First Fleet re-enactment in Sydney Harbour on Australia Day, the opening of the new Parliament House in Canberra by Queen Elizabeth II, and the staging of World Expo '88 in Brisbane. For many Indigenous Australians, Phillips's landing was an invasion to be marked not by celebration but by mass protest for the 'Year of Mourning', a term harking back to the 1938 protest against Australia's 150th anniversary festivities. On 26 January, over 40 000 people marched in Sydney in the nation's biggest demonstration since the Vietnam moratorium. Indigenous activist Burnum Burnum symbolically claimed England by planting the Aboriginal flag on the cliffs at Dover. And in 1987, poet, writer and activist Kath Walker had returned her 1970 MBE in protest against the bicentennial and adopted a traditional name, Oodgeroo Noonuccal.

The Australian Government was not completely immune to the issues underlying the protests. On 12 June 1988, prime minister Bob Hawke attended the annual Barunga cultural and sporting festival in a small Indigenous community south of Katherine in the Northern Territory. During his visit, the chairmen of the Central and Northern Land Councils, Wenten Rubuntja and Galarrwuy Yunupingu, presented Hawke with a petition framed by bark paintings. Known as the Barunga Statement, it was based on the earlier bark petition sent by the Yolngu people in 1963. The Barunga Statement called for recognition of land rights and a formal treaty with Indigenous people. Hawke accepted the petition and promised a treaty by 1990. The promise fuelled some optimism but has never been fulfilled.

Despite the huge protests and Hawke's promised treaty, Caroline Martin remembers feeling despair during the bicentenary celebrations. A Boonwurrung woman from Victoria, Martin 'just felt a real sense of hopelessness'. She was a descendant of a long line of strong women who had worked to better the rights and lives of Indigenous Australians, and was vice-president of the Dja Dja Wurrung Aboriginal Co-operative in Bendigo that her mother, Aunty

Carolyn Briggs, had helped establish. Well versed in the history of the Aboriginal rights movement, and committed to working with and for her community, Martin found few reasons to expect a better future. Yet while many Australians partied on, the protests and other actions – such as John Pilger's bicentennial documentary films *The Secret Country: The First Australians Fight Back* (1985) and *The Last Dream* trilogy (1988) – were furthering international knowledge of the history and ongoing discrimination faced by Indigenous Australians. And it was the knowledge of those overseas that would jolt 25-year-old sports photographer Wayne Ludbey into a new awareness of past and current racial wrongdoings.

. . . . . .

International civil rights activists had long been aware of the plight of Aboriginal people, as Australian historian Henry Reynolds discovered in London in the 1960s when a soapbox speaker at Hyde Park Corner put a gaggle of heckling Aussies in their place by reciting a litany of Australian racial abuses. The West Indian who confronted Ludbey in London at the pool in 1988 two decades on was similarly knowledgeable, likely from media attention to events like the bicentenary and the 1982 Commonwealth Games. Ludbey had been sickened by racism towards migrants in the 1970s. And while he had learnt about Aboriginal resistance in his final year of school in 1981, like most white Australians he had no special awareness of the contemporary problem in Australia. He was a young, long-haired 'snapper', focused on forging a career with the *Age* and enjoying life and the opportunities coming his way. Ludbey's press career had an almost accidental beginning. He recalls a conversation with his father when he was finishing high school at Kingswood College. 'My old man said, "What are we going to do with you?" I replied, "I don't know". He said, "What do you like?"' Ludbey responded that he liked photography and 'for some reason' added that he also thought he might become a chef. 'He said, "You're not being a chef".' Instead, his father got Wayne a job in 1982 as a cadet photographer for a group of Melbourne suburban newspapers.

As a cadet, Ludbey was a bit of a tearaway, smashing cars and accidentally setting fire to the darkroom – 'all those things you do when you're eighteen'. But he became good at his craft, and in 1984 at age 21 moved to the *Age* as a D-grade photographer. He'd wanted to work there, and it was a good fit straightaway. The *Age* was 'just a really great place to work. People were nice, there was an honesty about it, there was a truthfulness about it. It was just a great paper, you know'. The job also brought opportunities. Editor Michael Gordon encouraged him onto sport. This was a major breakthrough for the football-loving Ludbey, and while he initially felt out of his depth he was promoted in 1987 as the *Age*'s sports photographer. His shot of Carlton's Stephen Silvagni's mark of the year in the round 14 game against Collingwood in 1988 is one of his stand-out pictures from that period.

Ludbey's holiday encounter with the West Indian at a London swimming pool in 1988 came like a bolt from the blue, giving him new insight as he documented sport and other aspects of Australian social, cultural and political life. 'It was like an awakening, because I had no idea what he was talking about but he just talked about how badly white people treated Aboriginal people and I remember going, "Hang on a minute!" I remember even getting changed and he was still rabbiting on about it. There was really a lot of passion in what he was saying. He seemed to know a lot. Like when I sort of tried to pick him up, he sort of recited all these things at me, which I thought, "Oh, shit ..."'

The memory stayed with Ludbey. In May 1989, he was covering a Geelong home game against St Kilda at Kardinia Park. Nicky Winmar had a free kick for goal from the boundary line near where he was sitting. Maybe Ludbey was more aware of crowd noises having been away, for now he heard the vile abuse that so often came Winmar's way. A shocked Ludbey felt sick and ashamed. 'I'd never heard it before.' The Geelong barrackers 'really ripped into him about being black... I must say I felt nauseous'. Recalling his encounter in London, Ludbey thought, 'fucking hell, that guy is right'. For the first time, he realised something of the pressure that black players were under. The knowledge became a part of his psyche, something stored away, just like his awareness of when Gary Ablett Senior might fly for a 'screamer', or when David Parkin's jugular looked like it was about to burst.

. . . . . .

John Feder didn't have a pivotal moment like Ludbey's encounter with the West Indian in London. As the son of an Italian migrant father, and once the subject of childhood ethnic slurs himself, Feder was always aware of issues of racism. But initially Melbourne seemed free of that, and Feder set off to pursue a career in photography. It was not to be a straightforward path.

In 1982, having just finished school, Feder began a fine arts photography course at RMIT. With 'slap-dash bad habits' honed from snapping at the trots and at cars passing on the Princes Highway in Bulli, Feder was not easily moulded and left the course feeling disillusioned. His older brother, press photographer Tony Feder, found him work taking pictures for suburban papers, but John felt inexperienced and overwhelmed by the volume of work. Realising he needed a better foundation for his chosen craft, John applied for the physical education course at Footscray Institute of Technology. At the interview he stated upfront that he wanted to be a sports photographer rather than a teacher, and was surprised when he was accepted into the course. It was a sign the Institute was interested in educating people broadly.

The academic culture was wild as well as scholarly. Studies were punctuated by drinking games and pub crawls with staff and students on Friday afternoons. Among his fellow students at Footscray were Brian Wilson, Sean White and other VFL players. Every Saturday, though, no matter how big the night before, Feder worked at the racetrack, honing his skills by photographing the horses as they passed the 400-metre mark to document their relative positions. Eventually he was promoted to the finish line. Yet equally as important, his classes in the history and sociology of sport reminded Feder that the racism that had once affected him personally was still at work in the wider community. Later these classes helped him to 'look at football in a different way', but it was sport that was his passion at the time, not social issues.

Immediately after completing his Diploma of Education in the mid-1980s, Feder was offered a job as freelance sports photographer at the *Australian* and grabbed it with both hands. The bureau chief assigned him to cover the Australian Golf Open and liked his bold shots attained with the longer 400-millimetre lenses that were coming in at the time. Before Feder's arrival, the *Australian* typically used leftover shots from News Limited's Sunday papers, and he recalls the quality being 'ordinary'. Now, Feder would shoot a football game, develop the pictures, and choose high-quality original prints to go to the paper's Sydney press in the overnight bag from Melbourne. On assignments, he regularly bumped into fellow Aussie Rules fan Wayne Ludbey and they became friendly professional rivals. The two were among the youngest of the half dozen or so sports photographers active in Melbourne in the late 1980s, a group that included Ray Kennedy and members of the Bull clan.

In mid-1989, Feder was recruited to the just-launched *Sunday Herald* in Melbourne by Bill McAuley, a former colleague from the *Australian* who'd gone across to be the picture editor for the new venture. The *Australian* countered with an offer of a full-time job, but the *Sunday Herald* lure was too good to miss. The paper was well subsidised, and Feder revelled in the opportunity to travel weekly to profile a major sports star.

As a photographer in the 1980s, Feder covered all sports, but football was a favourite for the North Melbourne fan. He loved to watch the Krakouer brothers play. Though conscious at one level of the culture of racial abuse, like most non-Indigenous followers of the code in those days he did not heavily question it. 'If it happened now I'd be a lot more sensitive towards it. Back then I'd never condone it but I guess it was just part of the game.' And like many white Australians, he didn't personally know any Aboriginal people or know much about the deeper history of race relations.

Feder's racial awareness heightened when he returned to

Australia following a long break overseas after a year working at the *Sunday Herald*. The paper had folded while he was abroad, and he returned to a job at the *Sunday Herald-Sun*. One of his first assignments was a Collingwood versus North Melbourne game at Victoria Park. 'That's when it really struck me, how savage the crowds were. Just the language – women, men, didn't matter who.' Having worked in a pub and as a photographer in multicultural London, with friends from many racial backgrounds, he can remember 'just being totally shocked' by the language and the intimidating tactics of the crowds.

Just as it had for Ludbey at Geelong in 1989, the all-pervasive racism in football suddenly hit Feder that day at Victoria Park. The racism had long existed, but it was so common and familiar, so culturally accepted, that it hadn't made a deep impression. In this neither man was alone: most spectators and players simply were not attuned to the problems faced by Aboriginal players like Winmar and McAdam who regularly experienced racial abuse in their lives on and off the ground. For now, racism remained largely unremarkable and unremarked upon.

. . . . . .

Despite the ongoing racist abuse, both Nicky Winmar and Gilbert McAdam excelled in 1989. It was Winmar's best year to date. Imposing himself around the ground he had his most disposals to date, while kicking another 43 goals. This time Winmar won the St Kilda best and fairest award, which had been renamed the Trevor Barker Medal in honour of the St Kilda champion's retirement that year. Tony Lockett once again benefited from Winmar's precise delivery. After nine games, Lockett had 78 goals and the Saints were challenging for the top five. But injuries and suspensions derailed Lockett and St Kilda's season, and they only won another three games for the year. Winmar's brilliance led to 16 Brownlow votes, equal third. But he ended the year yearning for team success.

McAdam's 1989 season was also the best in his even shorter career. Neil Kerley played McAdam wherever he needed a spark, from wing to ruck-rover to half-forward flank. Roaming far and wide, McAdam was able to run all day while still retaining the acceleration to dash away when needed. He complemented his running with high-quality skills and thrilling high marks, with his frequent goals and marking filling the weekly highlights package. One of the 'awesome foursome' together with fellow Indigenous players Phil Graham, Eddie Hocking and Derek Kickett, McAdam led Central District to a qualifying final which they lost to Port Adelaide. He not only won the Bulldogs' best and fairest, but became the first Aboriginal player to win the Magarey Medal, polling 23 votes. The immediate effect on McAdam was enormous. 'When I knew I'd won it, before the count was finished, I started crying straightaway because it just hit me emotionally.' Between luncheons and functions, wining and dining, he didn't sleep for three days.

Charlie McAdam was listening to the count on radio in Alice Springs. When Gilbert won, 'all his mates were crying'. The next morning, after a stream of visitors congratulated him as if he had won it himself, Charlie and his brother-in-law 'jumped in a car and drove down to Adelaide to congratulate him, and there were celebrations and carrying on – that was the proudest moment for us all'. Down in Adelaide, Val McAdam was 'crying like mad'. Elliot McAdam also wept as he saw the live footage. 'It wrenched you to bits', he noted, thinking back to all the hard times the family had endured.

Everyone wanted to speak to Gilbert McAdam in the days after he won the Magarey Medal. As journalists questioned him about his life, McAdam noted that some of his opponents had racially abused him over his career. The abuse had been strongest in his first year when he was still a relatively unknown player, and had lessened 'as his ability was recognised'. The comments created a furore in Adelaide. Calls were made for the South Australian Commission for Equal Opportunity to find ways of reducing racism on the football field. Commissioner Josephine Tiddy was happy to work with the SANFL, noting 'there was little doubt that racism occurred in football', but the SANFL 'believed the league's affairs should remain its own'. 'If players had a problem', the general manager, Leigh Whicker, suggested, 'they should take it up with their club so it could be brought to the attention of the board of league directors'. The controversy in Adelaide was largely ignored by the other states, and soon died down. It did, however, cause Paul Chamberlin, a journalist in Sydney, to ask whether new racial vilification laws just passed in New South Wales would cover sporting slurs. 'The acting president of the Anti-Discrimination Board, Mr Steve Mark, said calling someone a "wog" would not usually be considered an offence, but comments which incited hatred, serious contempt or severe ridicule could.'

A few months later, McAdam sweated it out to see if a team in the soon-to-be-rebadged AFL was going to draft him. He was still skinny and only about 67 kilos around that time, and wonders if those in Victoria felt he might struggle in their more ruthless game. In the second round St Kilda took the chance, choosing McAdam with pick 17. The first thing that came into Gilbert's head was 'Oh, wow, I'm going to be playing with Nick Winmar. I'm going to be kicking a ball to Tony Lockett. How good is that going to be? So when I first went there and met them all, it was like – oh, I was just – it was like I was in dream world. It was just unbelievable'. First, however, Gilbert McAdam would fulfil his contract with Central District and play out the 1990 season with them. That same year an incident of racist abuse would interrupt Nicky Winmar's career.

. . . . . .

Waverley, 1990. Saturday 11 August, Hawthorn versus St Kilda. The Hawks were desperate for a win. Hawthorn's Dermott Brereton wrote in his regular *Sunday Age* column that weekend, 'This year, we can't afford to drop a game ... This year, we find ourselves playing for self-preservation'. The Hawks triumphed 119 to 83, but the game came to be remembered more for the way Nicky Winmar was involved in repeated skirmishes with Brereton. One reporter, trying to explain Winmar's actions, said they were 'born of frustration that would not normally surface if the footy was in his grasp'. Another picked up on something more complex but unexplained. 'And while Nicky Winmar would seem to have some explaining to do over several unscripted meetings with Brereton, Brereton may not emerge completely unscathed.' Two days later, Winmar was charged with kicking Brereton and assaulting him with a hand to the eyes and face, and was then suspended for ten games by the AFL tribunal.

What really happened on the field at Waverley that day in 1990 took several years to emerge. In 1998, Brereton wrote an article in the *Age* admitting that he had 'dedicated' the match to racially abusing Winmar when 'the ball was out of my area', with Nicky eventually retaliating. 'I was the one who should have received a penalty', admitted Brereton all those years later. Winmar, who'd pleaded not guilty to one of the charges, had not raised Brereton's abuse in his own defence in 1990, silenced perhaps by a system that tacitly condoned the culture of racism. Instead, he toed the line and apologised publicly to Brereton and to the AFL. Two days after the tribunal's verdict, a humour piece in the *Sunday Age*, which matched footballers with commercial products they could sell, paired Winmar with Telecom's *Yellow Pages* ('let your fingers do the walking') in reference to the assault. If this added insult to injury, Winmar also remained quiet. It was a punishing reminder of the deep racial injustices in the game.

Nicky Winmar playing for
St Kilda in 1992.

Gilbert McAdam playing
for St Kilda in 1992.

John Feder taking
a breather at the
1994 Commonwealth
Games.

John Feder's picture
of Nicky Winmar's
gesture, 1993.

Wayne Ludbey on the job.

Wayne Ludbey's picture of Nicky Winmar's gesture, 1993.

Two guilty: LA riot threat eases

By Chris Reed

Two policemen in the Rodney King beating case, the sergeant in charge and the officer who delivered most of the blows, have been found guilty. But the other two have been acquitted.

This verdict, brought in after one week of tense deliberations from a jury of eight men and four women, is regarded as likely to avoid a repeat of the mass riots that occurred last year when another jury acquitted the four.

That result, in a case brought by the state of California, provided riots to Los Angeles that killed 53 people and were the worst urban disturbances in America this century.

At the First African Methodist Episcopalian Church, a centre of black culture and politics in south-central Los Angeles, the black and Hispanic stars that felt the brunt of the riot last year, the congregation wept, swayed, prayed and praised the Lord. "It's right, it's right, it's only right," said one devotee before breaking down.

However, the case will not all now go away. Sergeant Stacey Koon, an officer with two maximum degrees who coolly testified that his officers' actions were justified in subduing the "drug-crazed giant" Rodney King, and Laurence Powell, who delivered most of the 56 blows on the notorious video tape of the beating, have received police union help to pay for their defence. They are almost certain to appeal.

Gino Ray, a neighbourhood activist, spoke for the militant view. She said: "Two out of four seems an experiment. I am happy for what we got, but we feel the two will never spend a day in jail because they will be appealing for years."

However, she added, she had expected a riot. The people had not 'planned' a riot last time, and there was no plan this time. There were also nearly 16,000 police officers on the streets and people did not have the will this time in rebel.

Sergeant Koon and Mr Powell face a maximum penalty of 10 years in prison and a fine of $US250,000. The sergeant, who late year published a book in the case in which he made overtly racist remarks — "but no money" according to his lawyer — because the key figure in the defence as the only man to take the witness stand.

In the California state case last year, three of the four officers testified. The mainly white jury accepted a defence argument that the graphic video tape upon which the prosecution relied almost entirely was not enough. In a ration paraoid about crime, that jury accepted that "the thin blue line" was all that remained between them and the rule of crime.

This time, the prosecution realised that the video tape was insufficient. A top Department of Justice lawyer from Washington led a team that prosecuted much more vigorously — but had a tougher case to prove. They had to show that the officers intended to deprive Mr King of his right to an orderly arrest when they stopped his speeding car after a chase just over two years ago.

● Continued P2

Ready for the worst: Californian National Guardsmen check their equipment. They are on alert and ready to move at 15 minutes' notice.

Shock swing to Libs in Qld poll

By Amanda Buckley, political correspondent

The fate of the federal Attorney-General-designate, Michael Laverich, was in the balance last night. The delayed Dickson election is likely to be decided by 4000 postal votes to be counted over the next week.

At close of counting Labor was about 470 votes ahead after a strong swing to the Liberals in rural areas of the north-eastern Brisbane seat. Late last night Labor's campaign director, Wayne Swan, predicted a narrow Labor win.

"It's very close but we think we will get there," said Mr Swan, the state secretary of the Queensland ALP and the newly elected member for the federal seat of Lilley.

The new seat would fall in the Coalition with a swing of 1.3 per cent. A long drought has been the big issue in outlying areas of the seat, and the Liberal candidate, Bruce Flegg, has claimed that the arrogance of Prime Minister Paul Keating is selecting Mr Lavarch's an Attorney-General-designate before he had won his seat had alienated voters.

The result of the election will not make much difference to the Government's comfortable 13-seat lead in the House of Representatives, but a Coalition win would help repair some of the damaged morale after its fifth successive election defeat.

If the Coalition wins, the Opposition Leader, John Hewson, can take no credit because he failed to appear in Dickson during the campaign.

The delayed election was caused by the death of a minor-party candidate in the lead-up to the 13 March general election.

Mr Lavarch, 31, would be the youngest federal minister yet if he was the seat. A former solicitor and the father of two, he held the neighbouring seat of Fisher until this election. His rival, Dr Flegg, 38, is a businessman and doctor.

If Mr Lavarch loses, the Prime Minister will be forced to make an embarrassing Cabinet reshuffle, and another Queenslander, possibly Con Sciacca or Gary Johns, would probably be elevated to the Ministry.

Mr Keating said last night he still expected Mr Lavarch to win. He congratulated Mr Lavarch on his good effort in a drawn-out and difficult campaign.

ANC two killed in protests

A white man yesterday shot dead two black demonstrators in the right-wing South African stronghold of Vanderbijlpark, raising fears of more racial attacks as protests continued over the slaying of Communist Party chief Chris Hani.

The killing of the two African National Congress supporters threatened to destroy a new found mood of discipline, echoed yesterday at the organisation's level, up to its promise of maintaining order during the mass demonstrations.

The shooting occurred as the ANC prepared to hold a mass vigil for Mr Hani in a stadium outside Soweto today and a funeral tomorrow near his home in Boksburg.

In Johannesburg 3000 heavily armed members of the security forces were on hand as more than 10,000 ANC supporters took to the streets, some carrying spears and stones.

ANC leaders appeal their pledge to ensure there was no violence.

● Full report, P9

Winmar: I'm black and proud of it

By Nick Place

Saint and sinner: Nicky Winmar responds to yesterday's racist taunts.

For St Kilda's Nicky Winmar, the moment of triumph over Collingwood yesterday meant the chance to confront those in the crowd who had hurled racial taunts.

After his fourth consecutive vote-winning performance, Winmar turned toward Collingwood supporters, pointed at his bared chest and declared: "I'm black — and I'm proud to be black."

Although many Aboriginal players tend to shrug off the racial abuse that appears to have become a feature of the game, Winmar's defiant gesture suggests a change in attitude that, for him at least, enough is enough.

As the siren signalled St Kilda's first win over the Magpies since 1979, Winmar stood in the forward pocket closest to the Magpie cheer squad, raised both arms and turned a full 360 degrees.

The 27-year-old then faced the Collingwood cheer squad and repeated edly raised and lowered his arms before lifting his jumper to reveal his stomach and chest.

Earlier, Winmar was believed to have been on the receiving end of racial abuse from the crowd at the Collingwood cheer squad's end of Victoria Park when he tangled with Magpie rover Tony Francis.

Sunday Age photographer Wayne Ludbey was among those close enough to hear his proud post-match declaration.

As the Magpie fans howled, Winmar saw them kisses before jogging to the centre of the oval to embrace another Aborigine, Gilbert McAdam, who was also among the Saints' best players.

St Kilda gathered to enjoy their first triumphant walk from Victoria Park in almost two decades, before leaving the oval in a huddle.

Predictably, Winmar was last off the field. He logged behind his teammates to blow some final kisses to the Collingwood supporters. Witnesses said some responded by spitting toward Winmar as he ran up the race. Winmar said after the match that he

had seriously considered leaving St Kilda for the West Coast Eagles at the end of last year.

During the 1992 finals series, Winmar said St Kilda officials had failed to drive him to hospital after he broke a collarbone. St Kilda repeatedly denied the allegation, but Winmar was clearly disenchanted.

In the end, he said he could not imagine playing against the Saints, and decided to stay.

St Kilda's shock victory was not the only surprise yesterday. Geelong, missing Gary Ablett, Mark Bairstow and Ken Hinkley, outran, outmanned and outgunned Hawthorn at Waverley Park to storm home by 40 points.

In the other match, North Melbourne continued to improve as a potential finals contender as it demolished Melbourne by 12 points despite easing off after halftime.

● Full reports, Sport (P3&)

She is 13. This Australian tourist has just bought her for the night

By Paul Robinson

On tour: Andrew, from Sydney, leaves a Bangkok bar with a girl of 13. He has been in the Thai capital for a week and says he has slept with three teenage girls who he says were "just gorgeous".
Picture: PAUL ROBINSON

Victorian and Federal police are closely monitoring the activities of travel agencies and more than 50 known paedophiles after the detection several organised sex tours to Asia.

The Victoria Police have a carefully infiltrated sex travel agency council by two men who home is in the northern suburbs of Melbourne.

The operation, code-named Smart, established that eight organised paedophiles were leaving a 26-day sex tour of Thailand. The operation faltered when Victoria police failed to get the co-operation, necessary overseas. The paedophiles excursion went ahead.

These travel agencies and paedophiles are still under surveillance. Their names have done little to Philippines authorities, who have hinted at least 10 Australians are alleged to be molesting Filipino boys.

Among those banned from a Philippines is a wealthy Tasmanian businessman who has written regularly to a Filipino youth aged 6 who was 15. The youth spoke in a Sunday Age letter in Manila last year confirming this sexual relationship and producing letters from a married man, sent in March a year ago.

The businessman, however, is based from Thailand and is known to Thai police. After becoming extensive Victoria Police surveillance, the man flew recently to Thailand with a male friend.

According to an unpublished Victorian police report on child prostitution in Asia, completed in April, a joint police-customs operation has also "uncovered a number of prominent (Australian) male travellers involved in an inter-national boys' association was were travelling to both Thailand and the Philippines and having sex at liaison with Asian boys of same age as those normally controlled by paedophiles are milled to their care in the young organisation".

The report also found that a large Victorian child pornography distribution racket shows strong links between Australia and the Philippines.

The Federal Government has long concerned about the involvement of Australians in the child sex trade since the former Minister for Health, Brian Howe, visited Thailand last year. Mr Howe advised the then Attorney-General Michael Duffy, who commissioned a report on the possible legal responses to Australian exploited children overseas.

Further action has been delayed because of the federal election, the retirement of Mr Duffy from Parliament and the delayed appointment of Queensland lawyer Michael Lavarche to the Attorney-General's position.

● Reports, pictures P4, P5. Editorial P17

The *Sunday Age* front page on 18 April 1993. The caption on the Winmar photo read 'Saints and sinners: Nicky Winmar responds to yesterday's racist taunts'.

Sunday
Herald-Sun

Sunday, April 18, 1993   90c

● Nicky Winmar, Russell Morris, Stewart Loewe and Danny Frawley celebrate yesterday's win.

NEW A-G IN FIGHT TO WIN SEAT

St Kilda ends Pie hoodoo

ST KILDA champion Nicky Winmar copped plenty of flak from the Collingwood cheer squad at Victoria Park yesterday. But, he had the perfect answer when the final siren sounded.

To salute the Saints hoodoo-breaking victory over the Magpies and silence the opposition fans, Winmar lifted his jumper and pointed to his stomach.

"We won with determination" was the St Kilda star's message to Magpie followers. Winmar was again one of the best players afield.

The Saints' win at the Magpie homeland was the first since 1976.

"If you can win here you can win a grand final," a jubilant Winmar said after the game.

Finally restoring order after several rousing renditions of When the Saints Come Marching In, coach Ken Sheldon described the players' effort as one of the best he'd seen.

Club president Travis Payze said it had been almost 30 years since he'd seen such a St Kilda effort.

But an unhappy Collingwood coach Leigh Matthews said the short-term break from Monday's clash at the MCG contributed to his team's performance.

● Full reports Pages 39 and 41

● Nicky Winmar gives Collingwood fans his own message: "We won with determination". Pictures: JOHN FEDER

6000 postal votes key

By PAT GILLESPIE and
MICHAEL McKINNON

THE five-week-old Keating Government received its first major setback last night with Attorney-General Michael Lavarch fighting to win the Dickson supplementary election.

The result in the new seat of Dickson will be decided by 6000 postal votes to be counted tomorrow.

Mr Lavarch was only 370 votes ahead of Liberal candidate Dr Bruce Flegg although the seat was seen as being marginally Labor.

Labor's new Attorney-General was on only 50.3 per cent of the vote to Dr Flegg's 49.7 at the close of counting.

If Mr Lavarch loses on postal votes, the immediate effect would be that Mr Keating would have to rethink his ministry which is just in the process of settling in to new positions.

● Continued Page 2

Skase: I need lung swap

● Report Page 11

LA RIOT FEAR AS 2 FOUND GUILTY — P7

WEATHER: Fine and sunny. Light winds and local sea breezes. EXPECTED TOP: 25. YESTERDAY'S TOP: 27. Details: Page 111

The *Sunday Herald-Sun* front page on 18 April 1993 (late edition). The caption on the Winmar photo read 'Nicky Winmar gives Collingwood his own message: "We won with determination"'.

Peter Nicholson's cartoon from the *Age*, 20 April 1993.

These striking stencils of Nicky Winmar appeared in Melbourne's Canada Lane (the artist is unknown).

Wayne Ludbey's photo of the AFL press conference with Michael Long, Damian Monkhorst and Ross Oakley on 5 May 1995.

Rocco Fazzari's cartoon from the *Sunday Age,* 9 May 1993.

Nicky Winmar and Gilbert McAdam at Victoria Park for the launch of the 2013 AFL Indigenous round.

Adam Goodes responds to racial abuse during the opening match of the 2013 Indigenous round.

4
Rising
concerns

*'I'd make a racist comment
every week if I thought
it would help'*

In late August 1991, Melbourne journalist Caroline Wilson
rang Gilbert McAdam. It was the eve of the finals, a series
that would include the Saints for the first time in almost
two decades. But Wilson wasn't calling McAdam to speak
about the way he and Nicky Winmar had helped St Kilda
climb into the top four. She was calling him to speak about
racism in Australian Rules football. Though it was Gilbert's
first season in the AFL, McAdam was 'fantastic' to talk to,
recalls Wilson. Already he had a reputation as an excellent
advocate for his people. McAdam 'was a really smart bloke
and he was very socially aware, very aware of his community and his role in the game'.

Along with informing Wilson of the state of play as he'd found it, Gilbert McAdam provided several key quotes for an article. McAdam was aware that some Australian states had been developing racial vilification legislation. But these developments didn't seem to apply to on-field incidents. 'Anywhere else you can take them to a court', he noted. 'On the footy field, who hears you? It really hurts us when they say things about our colour. As a white person, you can't know how much it hurts us. We're really proud of what we are.' It was the first time in Melbourne that a football player had publicly voiced the pain felt by Indigenous people, a pain sharpened by more than 200 years of dispossession, ridicule and mistreatment. For the abuse tended to imply that there was something wrong with being an Indigenous Australian. Something shameful; something inferior.

Wilson cited McAdam in an article that was published in the *Sunday Age* that week, but it was a quote from another player that resonated loudest and longest. That player was Tony Shaw. 'It's a business out there', the Collingwood captain had told Wilson when she asked him about racist abuse between players. 'I'd make a racist comment every week if I thought it would help win the game. If I think I can say something to upset someone, then I'll say it. I couldn't give a stuff about their race, religion or creed. If they react, you know you've got 'em.'

Wilson knew that many players were racially abusing Indigenous opponents, but Shaw's brutal honesty was the first time someone had admitted to it. She was sure she had a huge story. As she observed at the start of her piece, 'Racism has become a detested word in most circles but in League football, which insiders like to consider has become totally professional, there is disturbing evidence that on-field racist abuse has increased as the black influence has grown'. Wilson was quick to show the Shaw quote to the sports editor at the *Sunday Age* but recalls receiving a lukewarm response. For a while, the life of the article followed the familiar pattern of reporting on Australian race relations – it caused a bit of a stir, and then was forgotten.

It was a telling sign of the times. Indigenous affairs were starting to occupy a more prominent place in the popular imagination. Concern with racism in footy was also rising. But neither issue was yet large enough to lead to a substantive movement for change in the world of Australian Rules football.

. . . . . .

St Kilda had hoped Gilbert McAdam was the missing piece, the player who would bring the team back to glory. But his path to the club was delayed as he saw out the final year of his contract with Central District. While McAdam remained in Adelaide through the 1990 season, the Saints endeavoured to change their losing ways. Ken Sheldon was brought in as coach and instructed to remedy the culture of the club. St Kilda players had a reputation for partying long and hard, and Sheldon worked closely with football manager Peter Hudson to bring a more professional ethos to the club. The Saints started the 1990 season brightly, winning four of their first five, on the back of impressive performances from new recruit Jim Krakouer among others. They were in fifth spot in round 10. But their season was hampered by a serious knee injury to Tony Lockett and Nicky Winmar's later suspension. The Saints battled home, finishing ninth. Now they would get to see what was possible with McAdam in the squad.

Gilbert McAdam began the 1991 season in impressive fashion. Winmar and Lockett were both still out. But McAdam was unfazed. He had 32 possessions in the round 1 victory against Richmond, 29 in the subsequent loss to Geelong, and another 24 in the third round win against Melbourne. His first hiccup came in round 4 at Moorabbin Oval against Collingwood. The Magpies were coming off their first premiership victory in over 30 years – a period during which they had lost eight grand finals and which coined the derisive term 'Colliwobbles'. Led by their diminutive, aggressive captain Tony Shaw, the Pies were renowned for their toughness. Straightaway the Collingwood players greeted McAdam with racist abuse.

'Now, '91 when we played Collingwood, it started from the first time that we played them, this racism stuff', McAdam vividly recalls. 'I'll tell you right now, we got it straight on the field from the opposition players.' Though McAdam had been racially abused playing school footy in Adelaide and again in the SANFL, he'd never copped anything as bad as this from opposition players. 'I never heard anything like that before until I came to the AFL. It was really bad.' In that round 4 match McAdam struggled for the first time that season, gathering only 14 possessions. But the Saints fought hard. At half-time it was only their inaccuracy that limited their lead to 5 points. By the end of the third quarter Collingwood had a 1-point lead, though St Kilda had still taken four more shots on goal. In the last quarter however, it was Collingwood who squandered their opportunities, kicking 2 goals, 7 points to merely draw.

. . . . . .

R acial abuse on the footy field was nothing new, but it seemed to be increasing rather than declining. One possible reason was the upsurge in Indigenous Australians being recruited by VFL and then AFL clubs. Only eighteen Aboriginal men had played in the VFL from 1906 to 1980, but that number had more than doubled by 1991. Along with established players such as the Krakouer brothers, Michael McLean and Nicky Winmar, a host of young Indigenous players were beginning to emerge in 1991, including Gilbert McAdam, Michael Long and Gavin Wanganeen.

As the abuse on the field increased, off-field pressure was also building. At the beginning of the 1991 season an unidentified individual or group began a hate mail campaign against a number of young Indigenous players. The targets included Chris Lewis and Troy Ugle of the West Coast Eagles and Essendon's Michael Long and Derek Kickett. At once 'sadistic, violent and hurtful', the letters contained death threats and had 'devastating effects on the recipients'. Michael Long, who was already struggling to 'come to terms' with life in Melbourne, called on members of his family to come from interstate as a 'security precaution'.

Chris Lewis was affected similarly. Growing up in Perth, he was obsessed with footy. His father, Irwin Lewis, had played for Claremont but was better known as the first Indigenous Australian to attend an Australian university. All Chris Lewis could think about, though, was playing footy. Honing his skills in mad 'three on three' games played on a full-sized football ground, Lewis starred at every level. A founding member of the inaugural 1987 West Coast Eagles team, he had a dazzling first season. When he was named in the VFL's All-Australian team, the sky seemed the limit at first, but he struggled to cope with the racist abuse he encountered when playing in Melbourne.

Nicky Winmar, Derek Kickett and Maurice Rioli had all found racial abuse worse in Perth than Melbourne. Kickett remembers how he 'used to cop it every week in Western Australia'. Danny Ford, who coached Coolbellup in Perth, a team filled with Aboriginal players, was called racist names 'from crowds and rival players since I started playing in Kalgoorlie' in the early 1970s, when he was eleven. Yet Lewis had 'never really' encountered racism playing footy in Perth. Perhaps it was because he mainly played school footy before his single season in 1986 with Claremont in the WAFL.

The shock of the abuse in Melbourne hit Chris Lewis hard. Like Winmar, Lewis was quiet, but had an air of defiance. And like Winmar, by the early 1990s he was a marked man. As the Hawks' Dermott Brereton admitted in 1998, he and a select group of Hawthorn team-mates were given free rein to undermine both Lewis and Winmar with racial abuse. To those watching closely from the outside, the constant abuse seemed to eat away at Lewis.

Mick Malthouse was one of those who noticed the corrosive effects that racist abuse had on Lewis. The Eagles coach from 1990 to 1999, Malthouse had an in-house view of the process. Looking back, he was concerned that the Eagles failed to support Lewis more. 'We accepted it and we have got a lot to pay for that as a nation, as a league and as individuals. Football wore him down and from a young man, when I first got to that football club, with a beautiful, big smile ... that became more and more tested through his career. More the shame.' Wayne Ludbey expressed similar sentiments. The Western Australian papers paid Ludbey to photograph the Eagles when they were in Melbourne. And as he took pictures year after year he became distressed by what was happening to Lewis. 'When Lewis first started playing, he was just a really beautiful young boy who was a great footballer. God knows what he went through, but to see him ... He just changed. He became hard.'

Perhaps it was the effect of the hate mail, but 1991 seemed to be a tipping point for Lewis. For much of the season the West Coast Eagles were clearly the best team in the competition. Midway through the season, opponents began to see if stopping Lewis would clip the Eagles' wings. Martin Flanagan, a regular football journalist for the *Age*, recalled that Lewis went from being the best player in the country in 1990 to being 'embroiled in fights seemingly every time he went out to play' in 1991. One of those fights helped to focus attention on Lewis, but not necessarily in a helpful way.

The day was Saturday 6 July 1991. The Eagles were playing Melbourne at the MCG. It was Lewis's 85th league game. In the first quarter, Lewis and Demon Todd Viney fought in one of several heated incidents between the two that game. In circumstances that were never fully clarified despite being videotaped, Lewis bit Viney on the ring finger of the left hand. At the ensuing AFL tribunal, Bert Gaudion, Lewis's representative, pleaded for leniency on the basis of weekly 'verbal abuse' from the opposition. 'From the moment he stepped out on the field he was harassed and subjected to verbal abuse.' Still new to the League, the Eagles later admitted they'd decided to use the term 'verbal abuse' rather than 'racial abuse' for fear of being seen as interstate 'whingers'. But the tribunal was unconvinced that verbal abuse was significant provocation and suspended Lewis for three weeks. Concerned that the tribunal had overlooked Lewis's claim that the biting was accidental, the Eagles provided new medical evidence, but the original penalty stuck.

The Lewis–Viney clash was big news that week, but not the biggest footy story. The story making the front pages was the price gouging of fans at AFL matches – they were paying up to four times the normal cost for items like pies, chips and drinks. When the press did discuss the Lewis–Viney incident, the emphasis on biting and suspension and the refusal to name the problem as racial combined to focus attention negatively on Lewis. And when word leaked that Viney had undergone HIV tests following the bite, Lewis was again vilified. Racism was not publicly discussed.

. . . . . .

For a time the issue seemed to die down. Instead, the question was how much the Eagles might miss Lewis. Another question was whether St Kilda could make the finals for the first time in more than a decade. The Saints were playing the best they had for years. When Winmar and Lockett returned to the team in round 7, St Kilda crushed Adelaide by 131 points. Winmar had 33 possessions, Lockett 12 goals. The Saints won seven of the next nine games, losing only to Essendon and West Coast. But then they stumbled, losing three straight games. They'd been in a similar place a number of times in the past few years, flubbing a chance to make the finals and fading out of contention. This time, however, Nicky Winmar was determined to drag St Kilda into the finals. After a bye in round 20, the Saints won their last four games of the regular season. Winmar averaged more than 28 possessions in those games. He received Brownlow votes in three of them, and helped Tony Lockett break out of a mini-slump with the big forward kicking bags of 13, 10 and 11 goals during that period. McAdam had been producing consistently, if not starring, and also made some key contributions in the run home. Nevertheless, 'it was Winmar who got us to the 1991 finals, our first for 18 years', recalled Melbourne writer and Saints barracker Stephanie Holt.

As the finals approached, Caroline Wilson was one of many keen observers struck by the emerging importance of Indigenous Australians to the AFL game. Three of the six finalists were powered by young Indigenous players: West Coast with Chris Lewis, Peter Matera and Troy Ugle; Essendon with Michael Long, Gavin Wanganeen and Derek Kickett; and St Kilda with Winmar and McAdam. In 1982, while working at the Melbourne *Herald*, Wilson became the first woman to cover Australian Rules football. In 1989 she became the first woman to win the AFL's gold media award. Wilson was one of the first of a new era of journalists interested in the personal tales surrounding footy, not just the facts and figures. Now, working for the *Sunday Age*, Wilson recalled the Viney incident and began to investigate racism in footy. Her 1991 article was the first to report the death threats, and featured extensive comments from Gilbert McAdam decrying racism in football and Tony Shaw defending it.

Despite Shaw's admission that he would 'make a racist comment every week' if he 'thought it would help win the game', the reaction to Wilson's article was muted. She had raised the lid on racism, but not opened Pandora's box. Many others in the football industry didn't want to hear about it. The AFL refused to comment. Bill Deller, the director of umpiring, stated 'he had no knowledge of on-field racism'. And Wilson recalled that a number of other journalists were shocked that she would ring a footballer like Shaw 'and quote him as saying that'. Some even condemned her for exposing football secrets 'that no one really needed to know about'. It was like Wilson had broken a taboo that no one else was willing to touch. As a result there was no public scandal, no media debate, and no AFL inquiry. A few readers were shocked, but only six letters to the editor were published in the *Sunday Age* over the coming weeks. Five correspondents condemned Shaw's attitude and tactics, while one merely accused him of naivety for speaking so candidly to a journo.

. . . . . .

The 1991 finals series gained much greater attention than the swirling undercurrent of racism in the code. The AFL had expanded their finals to include six teams, but made the mistake of having the teams placed third and fourth play off in an elimination final, with the team finishing sixth only having to play the fifth team in the other elimination final. The fourth-placed Saints therefore faced off against third-placed Geelong, with the loser eliminated. The result was one of the greatest finals of the decade. Geelong had a star-studded that had who'd made the grand final two years before. In contrast the Saints had only three players that had played a final in the AFL/VFL. Yet the Saints kicked the first three, including a beauty by McAdam who won the ball on the wing before bursting away to goal from 40 metres. The Cats came back hard, kicking the next 5 to lead by 10 at quarter time. The Saints dominated the second quarter, with Winmar and McAdam prominent, and Lockett on fire. They kicked 6 goals to Geelong's 1, to be up by 19 points. The Cats came back hard again, and won a rollicking third quarter to take a 1-point lead into the last quarter. Now Geelong's experience came to the fore. The Saints began the quarter tentatively, and the

Cats made them pay. St Kilda rallied late, Winmar taking the mark of the game to complement his 27 touches, but their desperate sorties forward went unrewarded. Lockett had kicked 9 goals, almost half of which came via passes from Winmar. McAdam had 22 touches and 2 goals. But Geelong won by 7 points. McAdam still feels like the Saints should have won. Yet his lasting memory of the game is of how fierce and wonderful a contest it was. When he watches it on an old VHS tape, the match still stands up to today's contests. 'It was just one of the best games you'd ever see.'

In contrast, the 1991 Grand Final between West Coast and Hawthorn failed to live up to its pre-match billing. Playing in their first grand final, the Eagles raced out to an early lead, but Hawthorn slowly pegged them back, easing to a 10-point lead at half-time. The Hawks were the dominant team of the era. It was their eighth grand final match of the last nine seasons, and they used their experience to keep West Coast at arm's length before bolting away in the last quarter.

. . . . . .

The untold story of that grand final was one of racist abuse. Having got word from another team 'that "Lewy" had been put off his game by taunts, racially based', the Hawks vilified Chris Lewis at every opportunity. Apologising on national TV 20 years later in 2011, Dermott

Brereton noted that Lewis 'was our number one target. He was an extraordinary player. So we thought, "Anything to curb this bloke's brilliance"'. 'I profusely apologise for what we did in those days', stated Brereton. 'The extent that it hits home, we didn't understand.'

If Brereton had listened to Gilbert McAdam's comments to Caroline Wilson, or stopped to think about why Winmar and Lewis responded so strongly to his abuse, perhaps he might have understood a bit earlier. Chris Lewis also felt let down that the West Coast Eagles did not act out against the racism directed at him. 'I was a little bit disappointed that we probably didn't, as a club, push the issue a bit further. But I think it was one of those areas that we all didn't want to go to because it was a bit prickly.' As Wilson had earlier reported, the Eagles were said to have 'debated suggesting to the AFL that racist abuse become a reportable offence'. The club was divided by the issue, general manager Brian Cook explained to Wilson. 'On one side of the fence is the theory that racism is a part of life and the players just have to learn to cope with it. On the other side, you have to say that it is an unnecessary part of football that should be eradicated. Unfortunately, West Coast sits in the middle.'

. . . . . .

If the AFL community was not yet ready to engage with the issue of racism within its own ranks, broader events were nonetheless focusing national attention on Australia's race relations. One of the most popular Australian songs of the year was Yothu Yindi's 'Treaty', which was particularly notable for its use of Yolngu language. Led by the Yolngu singer Mr M Yunupingu, Yothu Yindi had worked with Paul Kelly and Peter Garrett to write a song about the failure of the Labor Government to honour its 1988 promise for a treaty. A dance remix of the song by Filthy Lucre spent 22 weeks in the Australian charts and reached the number 6 position on the international Billboard dance charts.

The movement for Aboriginal land rights was also taking place in the nation's courts and parliamentary chambers. Aboriginal land rights issues and legal cases had begun decades before but had reached a symbolic high point in 1982 when Eddie Mabo and four other Meriam people from Mer, or Murray Island, in the Torres Strait turned to the High Court of Australia for recognition of their traditional land rights. As the case unfolded over the next ten years, the prospect of native title stoked fears among some sectors of Australia about possible land claims by Indigenous groups should Eddie Mabo win the day. A headline of an article that appeared in the same *Sunday Age* as Caroline Wilson's 1991 story fed the alarmists: 'Bill would give blacks State land'.

On 3 June 1992, the Australian High Court handed down its famous Mabo ruling that Torres Strait Islanders had historic rights to land. The doctrine of *terra nullius* –

that Australia was an empty land when the British arrived in 1788 – was finally overturned. Though specific to Murray Islanders, the ruling had implications for all Aboriginal and Torres Strait Islander people. It was widely celebrated by Australia's Indigenous communities, offering new hope that their long-standing ties to the land might also be formally recognised. The ruling also forced many non-Aboriginal Australians to reconsider their relationship to the land. It was a time of intense discussions between Indigenous and non-Indigenous Australians. Paul Stewart, a Taungurong man from Central Victoria who'd grown up in Collingwood, remembers that he 'kept getting asked' if he was going to steal the backyards of the white folk he knew. Stewart was only seventeen and used to joke with those who seemed scared by Mabo. 'I said, you beauty, we'll play the history of invasion the other way – just leave a pool in the backyard or something.'

．．．．．

In 1991, however, Stewart was more interested in the footy than in the implications of Mabo. The previous year, the drought-breaking premiership victory of his team, Collingwood, had led the club to act out a symbolic burial of the Colliwobbles in a ritual indicating that their dominance of the competition would now be unhindered. Despite their optimism, Collingwood then suffered the indignity of missing the finals in 1991. When the Magpies finished the 1992 regular season with sixteen wins, equal highest in the competition, Stewart and other Pies barrackers were thrilled that the team seemed to be back on course. Yet life for Collingwood was not yet perfect. Geelong and Footscray also had sixteen wins, and courtesy of a better percentage, finished in first and second position, ahead of Collingwood in third place. The AFL had improved its final-six system, with the team in third place now playing the team in sixth. In 1992, that side happened to be St Kilda.

The Saints' 1992 season had been mixed. Nicky Winmar and Tony Lockett again excelled, as did a young Robert Harvey. Winmar had almost a hundred more possessions than in any previous season, along with 55 tackles and the mark of the year. Lockett kicked 132 goals, while Harvey averaged more than 28 touches per game. Gilbert McAdam missed the first half of the year with a lingering groin injury, but was a strong contributor for the rest of the season. Yet despite these performances, St Kilda again struggled to finish out the season, winning only four of their last eight games to drop from third to sixth. They only scraped into the finals when Carlton lost their last match. St Kilda's most compelling match of the regular season had come in the one encounter they'd had with Collingwood.

Held on Monday 8 June, the Queen's Birthday public holiday, the game was played on a sodden MCG in front of more than 80 000 spectators. The Saints had all the play early, but were missing Tony Lockett and squandered their opportunities. Though they had eleven scoring shots to two, St Kilda were only up by 14 points at quarter time. The second quarter was more even and the teams headed to the half-time break with the Saints leading by 13. But the teams didn't get off the field for some time. The Collingwood players and many fans had again been racially abusing Winmar, McAdam and St Kilda's other Aboriginal player, Dale Kickett. Shaw kept going after the half-time siren, sparking a brawl involving 34 of the 36 players on the field. As the fighting ended, St Kilda coach Ken Sheldon had to usher McAdam 'away from the Collingwood players' race'. When the teams came back onto the field the game was ferocious. One scribe likened the match to 'trench warfare', noting that some recent grand finals 'have been played and watched with less intensity than this particular game'. Collingwood narrowed the deficit to a point by the end of the third quarter, and in the final quarter continued to grind the Saints down. They kicked the first two goals, taking the lead for the first time. But Winmar went forward and kicked a goal, Craig Devenport snapped another, and the Saints held on for a famous 1-point lead. McAdam had been superb, creating play from the backline, and Winmar had been magisterial all over the ground. The triumph was encapsulated in a picture of Winmar, McAdam and Kickett arm-in-arm taken after the game, but again media reports skirted around the issue of race.

Despite the Saints' victory in June, Collingwood were overwhelming favourites in the elimination final against St Kilda that September. By now the rivalry between the two teams was intense. 'We hated each other with a passion', noted McAdam. The shared hatred led to another fierce struggle. This time the game was even from the start. Lockett was being quelled by Gary Pert, while the Collingwood forward line also struggled. The result was 'a classic defensive struggle – a heavy, potent glass of red wine, a concoction developed by rivalry', observed sports writer Gerard Wright. The Saints led by a point at quarter time, squeezing that out to 13 points at half-time on the back of their other tall-forward, Stewart Loewe. The teams traded blows for the third quarter before the Saints blew the game open at the start of the final term. Lockett was finally breaking free, and three quick goals took St Kilda out to a 31-point lead twelve minutes into the term. But then the Saints relaxed and let the Magpies back in. Three goals to forward Ron McKeown and another to Scott Russell and the Pies were back within 8 points. Time, as much as the Saints themselves, conspired to stop Collingwood getting any closer, and they lost by the 8-point margin.

It was a tremendous upset, St Kilda's first finals victory for almost two decades. Collingwood had entered the finals full of expectation only to find themselves eliminated in the first game. Now, though, the Saints had expectations of their own, always a dangerous transition and one in which they lost focus. In the ensuing semi-final against Footscray, St Kilda were smashed in the opening term and never recovered. Nevertheless, the Saints appeared to be building to something. With a young squad they remained full of hope. In addition, Winmar and McAdam could enjoy the fact that they'd beaten their fierce rival Collingwood twice. Players from other teams such as Hawthorn had racially abused them, but Shaw's comments in 1991, and the brawl and then elimination of 1992, had made the Magpies their biggest adversary.

. . . . . .

The rivalry between St Kilda and Collingwood would reach a crescendo in early 1993, the International Year of the World's Indigenous People, when Winmar and McAdam next played against the Magpies, this time at Victoria Park. Even before New Year's Eve revellers around the country had ushered in 1993 with fireworks displays, the year had started with a bang. On 10 December 1992, prime minister Paul Keating had delivered his now-famous Redfern Address to launch the celebrations for the forthcoming year. The location was the inner-city Sydney suburb of Redfern, a place with strong historical importance to its large Aboriginal population. In his speech, Keating acknowledged that:

We took the traditional lands and smashed the
traditional way of life.
We brought the diseases. The alcohol.
We committed the murders.
We took the children from their mothers.
We practised discrimination and exclusion.
It was our ignorance and our prejudice.

The prime minister predicted that 1993 'will be a year
of great significance for Australia. It comes at a time when
we have committed ourselves to succeeding in *the test which
so far we have always failed*'. That test was the development of
Australia as a true social democracy, with 'opportunity and
care, dignity and hope' extended to all Australians equita-
bly. He acknowledged contributions made by Indigenous
Australians in many spheres, including sport, and called
upon white Australians to 'Imagine if our feats on sporting
fields had inspired admiration and patriotism and yet did
nothing to diminish prejudice'.

Keating spoke directly to a predominantly Aboriginal
audience assembled in Redfern Park, but his words resonated widely. An *Age* editorial called it 'frank and forthright', and noted its symbolic importance. His message
also echoed stirringly down the years. In 2007, ABC Radio
National listeners nominated his address as the third most
unforgettable speech of all time, behind Dr Martin Luther
King, Jr's 1963 'I have a dream' and Jesus' 'Sermon on

the Mount' but ahead of Churchill's 'We shall fight on the
beaches', Lincoln's Gettysburg Address and Kennedy's 'Ask
not what your country can do for you, ask what you can
do for your country'. Gilbert McAdam speaks for many
Aboriginal people when he describes the impact the speech
had on him: 'Mate, that was powerful. I remember it really clearly ... I felt pretty emotional when he said it, because
the points that he said ... just hit the nail on the head.
Oh, it was brilliant'. For Caroline Martin, the Mabo High
Court decision and Redfern Address were wonderful ton-
ics to the despair brought by the bicentenary celebrations.
'I felt that something was shifting, that there was a way
forward.'

Australia's celebration of the International Year of the
World's Indigenous People continued with the announcement by the Federal Government on 26 January 1993 of Mr
M Yunupingu as Australian of the Year for 1992. Two days
after Yunupingu's award, on 28 January 1993, Australia
recognised the authority of the United Nations Committee
on the Elimination of All Forms of Racial Discrimination
to receive and consider complaints from Australia. Yet if
things in Australia were shifting on a more general cultural
and legal level, the shift was yet to reach into the world of
footy.

On Sunday 28 March, Essendon played West Coast at Subiaco Oval in Perth in the match that concluded the first round of the 1993 footy season. Despite playing alongside Aboriginal team-mates Chris Lewis and Peter Matera, West Coast captain John Worsfold tangled with Essendon's Michael Long, 'quietly' sparking a season that would be dominated by questions of racism. While Worsfold later 'denied saying anything that could have been interpreted as racist', Long responded as if he had been vilified, punching the Eagles captain. As had often been the case in the first few years of his AFL career, Long was reported and suspended for the action. Once again, media reports contained no suggestion of verbal provocation or racial slurs by Worsfold. It was enough to lead Essendon's new president – David Shaw (no relation to Tony) – to make a stand. Something had to be done, he felt, before racism led Long and other Indigenous Australians playing for the Bombers to abandon the sport. In his debut presidential speech the following week, Shaw implied racism was central to Long's offence. The game was battling an increasingly ugly element of on-field racial slurs, he warned. 'I'm saying it because we have four or five Aboriginal guys and they cop heaps … It's quite obvious [the offenders] can't beat them on their own merits', he continued, 'so they have to try other tactics to counter them'.

David Shaw's ire captured media attention. Referring to his speech, the *Sunday Age* called racial abuse 'Football's black mark' and urged that on-field abuse be 'wiped from the game'. The legendary Noongar footballer, Syd Jackson, who played for Carlton from 1969 to 1977, weighed into the issue with an opinion piece in the *Sunday Age*. 'I was surprised and disappointed', began Jackson, to read 'that racism is as much a part of the game as ever. I had hoped that in the days since Polly Farmer, myself and a few of the others who played before us, that the public would have become used to seeing a lot of Aborigines playing. They know what champions they are and I would have thought they would show more respect.' Jackson had also hoped 'that footballers had become more understanding, more professional and better educated and would not feel the need to stoop to these tactics'. Aboriginal players already had an enormous burden placed upon them as role models by their own communities who wanted them – *needed them* – to succeed. Racism was too heavy an additional weight. While urging players to turn the other cheek, Jackson acknowledged that sustained abuse would lead to retaliation, and called for action. Specifically, he urged the AFL tribunal to take seriously the defence of racial sledging, and called upon the AFL itself to consider introducing a code of conduct to censure racial abuse.

In his Redfern Address, Paul Keating had called for the need for 'practical building blocks of change' to address injustices against Indigenous Australians. He cited the Mabo judgment as one of those building blocks. Yet for

change to occur, the problem of racism first had to be recognised officially. As in 1991 with Caroline Wilson's story,
the lid was again being lifted on racism in the AFL. The
question was, would anybody be able to rip the lid off this
time once and for all and make those in charge of the AFL
recognise the need for change?

. . . . . .

By April 1993, issues of race relations were starting
to dominate the Australian media, but they weren't
Australian issues. Instead, the focus was on South Africa
and the United States. By 1990 the decades of external and
internal pressure against the apartheid policies of South
Africa, including sporting and trade boycotts, had become
too much for the South African Government. Nelson Mandela, leader of the African National Congress (ANC), was
released from prison on 11 February 1990 after three decades of internment, and bans were lifted on anti-apartheid
groups. Mandela's release was greeted with fanfare and
hope around much of the world. But the transition to allowing black South Africans the vote and other civil liberties
was not seamless. April 1993 was a time of race riots, with
concerns growing that South Africa might be consumed by
a civil war.

At the same time, large-scale violence around race was a
concern in the United States. On 3 March 1991, an African

American man named Rodney King was beaten by police officers following a road chase in Los Angeles. The incident was videotaped by an onlooker and broadcast to public outrage. The assault, and subsequent trial of the police, exacerbated racial tensions in southern California. When four of the officers were found not guilty at the end of April 1992, Los Angeles was consumed by the largest race riots in America's history. Lasting for six days and resulting in the deaths of 53 people, injuries to 2000 others, and unprecedented property damage, the incident stunned the international community. And in April 1993, fears were being raised of further riots, for now a further civil trial of the police officers was just about to conclude.

On Saturday 17 April 1993, the two Melbourne Sunday papers were preparing front pages that provided updates on the riots in South Africa and the trial of the police officers in Los Angeles. Soon, however, two photographers would begin pushing for another image of race to take centre-stage – an image that would reverberate through much of Australia. For the Australian Rules football game that day between St Kilda and Collingwood had sparked a major race-related protest of its own.

5
The
match

*'Time for a
statement'*

On Saturday 17 April 1993, Gilbert McAdam stepped onto
Victoria Park for the first time. It was a shocking moment.
The Collingwood cheer squad was positioned next to the
players' race, the away team's entrance to the field. Opposing players had the daunting experience of walking right
past them. Among other things, the Magpies faithful would
spit and pour drinks on those walking past. And on this day
the crowd was thirsting for revenge. St Kilda had eliminated Collingwood from the finals the previous season. Now
the Magpies had the chance to repay the Saints, a club that
had last triumphed at Victoria Park seventeen years ago.
And the spiteful Pies crowd was keen to participate in the
revenge.

It was 90 minutes before the main game began, half-time of the Reserves contest that at the time still preceded senior matches. As usual, McAdam had walked out onto the ground with Nicky Winmar to 'suss out' what the ground was like that day, to see how wet it was, test the wind, gauge the hardness and consistency of the surface, and get a sense of how balls were bouncing off the ground.

As soon as the cheer squad saw McAdam and Winmar they started in, 'really giving it to us' as McAdam recalls. They were 'calling us petrol-sniffers, abos, coons – they were just calling us everything'. This was Winmar's fifth visit to Victoria Park, but the first time for McAdam. Abuse was common at other grounds. Kardinia Park in Geelong, for instance, was also notorious among Indigenous players. But here the set-up was particularly intimate and intimidating. McAdam was surprised by the way 'we were right in their space and they were right in our space'. It meant the abuse was more personal and direct than elsewhere 'which is probably smart, but wasn't smart for them that day because it got us pumped up'.

At first the intensity of the abuse just made Gilbert McAdam angry, like it had done with his father. Then it spurred him to action. Maybe it was the presence of his dad in the crowd, or the debate that had restarted about racist abuse in footy, or the discussions of land rights in Australia and civil rights around the world, that led to what happened next. Gilbert McAdam calmed himself down and decided that now was the time for a response. 'I got a bit angry when they started at us. Then I said to myself, "It's no use being angry". So when I got to the centre, I grabbed Nick and said, "Bro, we have got to do something today. We have got to make a statement. We'll show this mob, we'll make them quiet today". So who knows, I didn't know it was going to happen, but it happened!'

. . . . . .

Paul Stewart, by now an 18-year-old, was sitting close to the cheer squad, thinking that he used to be one of those 'little shits that hang around that race, just booing the opposition players'. His dad had put him in the cheer squad as a young kid. On match days Paul's uncle would throw bean bags in the back of a big truck, then Paul and a heap of other Koori kids would jump in and head down to Victoria Park. From the time of Doug Nicholls and before, the neighbouring working-class suburbs of Collingwood and Fitzroy had been the places where Victoria's Aboriginal peoples settled when they came to live in Melbourne. Australian Rules football quickly became a core part of community life. The Fitzroy Stars Football Club was established by community members in the early 1970s and many became passionate supporters of the Collingwood and Fitzroy VFL footy teams of those suburbs. Sitting as a kid in the cheer squad, Paul could see his dad and his uncle in the social members area just behind him, while his aunties and cousins sat in the outer and under the scoreboard.

Paul remembers as a kid yelling out at opposition players, telling them he hoped they'd lose. But now, in 1993, a number of those around him were screaming out that McAdam and Winmar were 'black bastards'. And worse. At the time he didn't think 'much of it' – racist abuse was one of the elements of the game, and it didn't seem like you could stop it. 'What do you do, what do you do?' Paul's outlook was changing, though. He'd started a TAFE course that was inspiring him to think about Australian race relations. And the events of that day in 1993 would become a turning point in his relationship with Australian Rules football.

It's likely that not everyone at the ground was aware of the abuse being directed at Winmar and McAdam. Though he missed the match, Troy Austin had 'never really felt a sense of racism in the environment' at Victoria Park. A Gunditjmara man whose Indigenous family hailed from western Victoria, Austin would find a spot at the Dights Falls end of the ground with many members of his family and friends. Austin felt pretty fortunate to grow up in the Fitzroy-Collingwood area among the strong Indigenous community around there. His dad, Jock, had helped establish the Fitzroy Stars Aboriginal Community Youth Club Gymnasium in 1982 and worked to re-establish the Fitzroy Stars Football Club in 1984 with the then 15-year-old Troy playing in the seniors. Going to the Pies games helped Troy feel like he belonged to both the local Koori and broader Collingwood communities. Looking back, it seemed to Troy that there were 'two different sections' at the ground: the members in the social club, and the 'knockabouts enjoying the footy' at the Dights Falls end of the ground.

In this other section, though, the racism was unavoidable. 'Danny Boy', a St Kilda supporter at the game, felt threatened by the venom and vitriol being directed at Winmar and McAdam. Another Saints barracker 'left the ground horrified and scared, and embarrassed to be a football supporter'. 'Shoot him. He is only a black' was the 'worst of many racial taunts that she heard on Saturday'. Sitting in the Social Members area near the cheer squad, Andrew Jackomos was also appalled by the intensity of the abuse. Andrew's father, Alick, was the son of Greek immigrants to Melbourne, and had married Merle Morgan who, like Doug Nicholls, came to Melbourne from the Cummeragunja mission. Alick and Merle became heavily involved in the Aboriginal rights movement, with Alick working as a field officer for the Aborigines Advancement League and spending many a Saturday afternoon with Nicholls gathering petitions calling for a referendum. Andrew had followed his father both in his passionate support for Collingwood and commitment to Indigenous rights. By 1993, he was the Victorian manager of the Aboriginal and Torres Strait Islander Commission. He remembers being 'uncomfortable' with the racist abuse that Magpies supporters had yelled at Syd Jackson in the 1970s, but Jackomos was just a kid then. Now the vilification of Winmar and McAdam made him question why he was at the footy. 'That day was just more intense, and the racism was more intense than it normally was from the Collingwood supporters. Looking around me in the social club I thought, "Do I really want to be like those people?"'

. . . . . .

St Kilda came into the game as clear underdogs. Despite having beaten Collingwood in both their games the season before, the Saints hadn't won at Victoria Park for 17 years. And the Magpies had begun the 1993 season in compelling fashion. Undefeated, they'd beaten the two teams that had finished above them in the 1992 regular season: Footscray and Geelong. The previous Monday the Magpies had also taken care of Essendon, another 1992 finalist, in convincing fashion in front of 87 000 spectators. Collingwood were missing their talismanic skipper, Tony Shaw, but St Kilda were without Tony Lockett. Yet the Saints came into the game with decent, if not inspiring, form. After losing their first match to Geelong, they'd then had a narrow victory over North Melbourne before steamrolling Sydney.

Gilbert McAdam had begun the season well but it was Winmar who was grabbing the headlines. The media had adjudged him St Kilda's best player in each of their first three matches and he was an early season favourite for the Brownlow Medal. The match against Collingwood would give both Winmar and McAdam a further chance to show-case not just their amazing skills but also the strength of their characters, will and courage.

. . . . . .

B eginning in front of a packed crowd on a beautiful clear day, the game was intense from the start. The first kick was smothered, the second was a kick off the ground and then Gilbert McAdam flew in from the half-forward line to lock the ball up. McAdam got the first clean possession from the resulting bounce, handballing to Nicky Winmar who kicked the ball into the Saints' forward line where a further ball up ensued. McAdam once again won the clear-ance, flinging the ball onto his boot but sending it left for a point. The Saints cut off the Collingwood forward sortie that followed, with Winmar switching play from the flank to the middle of the ground with a precise kick that broke the game open. Collingwood regained the ball deep in their defensive half, but after St Kilda big man Stewart Loewe smothered a handpass, the ball ended up with McAdam, who shimmied to his left before stepping to his right and kicking the goal from 45 metres out.

St Kilda continued to make the play, with McAdam

and Winmar in the thick of it. In the fourth minute, Winmar ghosted in to intercept and almost mark a dangerous Collingwood pass across the goal they were defending. As Collingwood regathered the ball and moved it forward, McAdam sprinted for 40 metres to bring down the Magpies' speedy rover Tony Francis from behind with a textbook tackle. The Pies barrackers were in full voice. Yet the St Kilda supporters who had journeyed across town were striving to match them, roaring in approval when McAdam slid forward shortly after to mark the ball at centre half-forward for the Saints.

McAdam and Winmar were in the thick of it all. At the eleven-minute mark of the quarter, McAdam flew high for what would have been a contender for mark of the year before dropping the ball, then bouncing to his feet and tackling the Collingwood player who roved it. Still, the Magpies were slowly working their way back into the game. Their big young forward Saverio Rocca was looking particularly threatening and he booted their first goal at thirteen minutes in after an impressive mark.

By midway through the first quarter the Saints had only a 2-point lead to show for their early dominance. Favoured by a light breeze, they were still playing with a desperation typified by McAdam, who smothered a Graham Wright kick out of defence and then gave away a 50-metre penalty for being overly attentive on the mark. But Collingwood had dropped a further player back into their defensive half and St Kilda lost their fluidity, bombing the ball long to contests where the Pies had the numbers.

The Pies started to take control of the game. When Rocca kicked his second they had the lead. Collingwood had a further opportunity immediately after but were denied by a marvellous Winmar tackle, followed straight after by McAdam running down another Magpie player. Now it was Collingwood's turn to squander their ascendency. Rocca missed a set shot from 20 metres out, directly in front. Barry Mitchell snapped the ball out of bounds on the full. And Robert Harvey blocked another shot on goal.

St Kilda's highlights continued to be largely the domain of Winmar and McAdam. In one sequence Winmar played on from a free in the back pocket. He kicked the ball to Sean Ralphsmith, received the handball running past, kicked to Stewart Loewe and kept running to receive a further handball that enabled him to deliver the ball into the Saints' forward fifty. He'd almost singlehandedly taken the ball the length of the ground. A few minutes later McAdam sharked a tap close to the Saints' goal, danced through the pack and snapped the Saints' second goal. McAdam then thanked the Collingwood ruckman Damian Monkhorst, giving him a light tap on the behind. The Magpies responded immediately, however, with Mark Fraser running into an open goal, and the first quarter ended with Collingwood up by 5 points.

. . . . . .

Collingwood began the second quarter with the breeze at their backs, but once it again it was St Kilda that came out the more ferocious of the two sides. In the first passage of play, Winmar battled the Magpies' Alan Richardson for possession of the ball on the wing, kicking and paddling the ball in front of him. Then, with Richardson retarding Winmar at the Saints' 50-metre line, McAdam burst through, picking up the ball and breaking away at speed. He steadied himself with a bounce and ran into the open goal. Less than 30 seconds had elapsed and the Saints were back in front, with McAdam having kicked all three of their goals.

One minute later the gangly Peter 'Spida' Everitt (playing just his fourth match) marked and goaled from 20 metres out after play had again been directed through McAdam. St Kilda were now 7 points in front. A Brad Rowe goal reduced the lead, but then Nathan Burke screwed the ball around his body to find the free McAdam, and Gilbert had his fourth goal of the game six minutes into the second quarter.

The intensity of the game was ratcheted up another notch as Collingwood began to match the endeavour of St Kilda, with both sides exerting tremendous pressure. By midway through the quarter the teams had traded goals. Winmar was imposing himself with some great tackles as well as precise kicks and had 10 possessions already. Robert Harvey, another emerging star for the Saints, had 14 touches. Then suddenly Harvey tore his right quadriceps and had to be carried off the ground. A few minutes later, Winmar gathered the ball singlehanded under intense pressure and kicked perfectly to set up another attacking move for the Saints. With St Kilda missing the run of Harvey, Collingwood started to gain the run of play. Yet despite kicking the next two goals, the Pies were squandering most of their opportunities, much to the frustration of the largely partisan Victoria Park crowd.

McAdam was being played up forward. With the ball mainly in Collingwood's half of the ground, he was denied the opportunity to impose himself as strongly on the game. But late in the quarter he received a handball among traffic in St Kilda's forward fifty. Deftly evading three opponents, he created space and sent the ball deep where Darren Bourke snared a vital goal. Magpie tall forward Ron McKeown answered with a goal of his own, and Collingwood went to the main break 58 points to St Kilda's 50. The crowd was grumbling, however, as the Pies had been wasteful in the last fifteen minutes, kicking 5:7 in the quarter as opposed to the Saints' 5:4.

Missing Lockett and now Harvey, and down at a venue where they hadn't won since 1976, the Saints were expected to fall away. Yet as they'd done in the previous two quarters, the Saints made a bright start to the third term. One minute in, Winmar sent another piercing kick forward to McAdam, who won a free. While McAdam missed his shot, and another a few moments later, St Kilda benefited from opportunistic snaps by Brett Bowey and Dean Anderson to retake the lead. Then came one of McAdam's best moments of the game. Collingwood's Alan Richardson was caught with the ball in the centre of the ground. McAdam swooped in to pick up the ball at pace, ran straight down the ground, bounced it twice. And drilled a goal from 55 metres out.

The Saints had kicked three goals in the first four minutes and their supporters were humming, with some starting up a St Kilda chant. When McAdam received the ball shortly after, the crowd buzzed in anticipation, then sighed in disappointment when he fumbled, only to crescendo again when he regathered and slipped two tackles. But a moment later, when Winmar received a free on the boundary next to the Magpies' goal, there were howls of abuse from the Collingwood barrackers in the crowd behind him.

The Saints were slicing through Collingwood. With McAdam now playing on the ball he again wowed spectators, weaving in and out to oohs and ahhhs from the crowd and gasps from the TV commentators, showing the form that had won him the Magarey Medal in Adelaide. Another goal had St Kilda up by 19 points and the Magpie crowd babbling with frustration. Angst soon turned to rage when St Kilda captain Danny Frawley collected the head of Michael Christian with his hip, knocking him out. Mick McGuane kicked a goal from the resultant free kick and the Pies were looking to come back like they had in the previous two quarters.

Now, however, Winmar elevated his game to another level. He drove the ball forward from the ensuing centre bounce and Bowey snapped a goal. The next centre bounce led to a similar Winmar clearance and the ball ended up with Everitt, who kicked a goal from deep in the right pocket. Soon after, Winmar delivered the ball forward again for a Dean Anderson mark. A straight kick made it three goals in four minutes, all from Winmar kicks into the fifty.

St Kilda were dominating now, but their next two shots hit the post. Bowey followed with a miss from 40 metres out, straight in front. At the 30-minute mark, with the ball on the Collingwood half-forward line, Winmar tackled first one Magpie player, then another, but hurt his back with the second tackle. With Winmar injured, the Pies kicked two quick goals to bring the lead back to 21. A sore-looking Winmar came back on the ground and courageously jumped in front of the oncoming Glenn Sandford to mark, receiving a clip on the head for his troubles. But Winmar was limping when the quarter ended soon after. St Kilda had kicked 7:7 but the late goals had given Collingwood 3:1 for the term. The Magpies were only 22 points down with the breeze at their back for the final quarter.

. . . . . .

The game tightened up again in the fourth quarter with the first fifteen minutes a dour affair brightened by another instance of McAdam evading three Collingwood opponents. Winmar was moving a little better and won a couple of frees, but St Kilda were now squandering their opportunities. After three behinds to the Saints, Gavin Brown kicked a goal midway through the term to bring the margin down to 19 points. Half a minute later and Brown had another, and the Magpies were within 13 with 10 minutes to go. A point to McKeown and a St Kilda turnover and now the Saints were only up by a goal.

St Kilda steadied with a Nathan Burke goal, the Pies answered with a long bomb by Shane Watson, and then Dean Rice ran into an open goal to put the Saints up by 12 points. Collingwood responded with a forward sortie yet could only get a point for their efforts. The Magpies were still in the game, only needing two goals to take the lead. Then, with three minutes to go, Nicky Winmar swooped on an errant handpass in the middle of the ground, ran to the fifty and slammed the ball through to seal the game. A mark on the goal-line by Stewart Loewe as the siren sounded, and the Saints were victorious by 22 points.

. . . . . .

In the time before the people of the Kulin nation had their lands taken away from them, Victoria Park was a sacred place and the site of corroborees – ceremonial meetings and festivals. Nicky Winmar knew this and was distressed by the way the ancient ground was now a site of racist abuse. It was the first time Gilbert McAdam had been on the receiving end of the venom of Collingwood barrackers at Victoria Park and it galvanised him with the desire to make a statement. Now McAdam and Winmar had made their statement on the field. They dominated the game to lead St Kilda to their first victory at Victoria Park since 1976. It was McAdam's best AFL game, and one of Winmar's most outstanding despite the back injury he received late in the third quarter. While they hadn't quite silenced the abusive mob of Magpie barrackers, McAdam and Winmar had snatched victory from them and roused the Saints' fans to gasp and cheer with joy. Andrew Jackomos still remembers how 'Nicky and Gilbert' had 'carved up Collingwood', while Paul Stewart recalls the way 'Gilbert flogged us'. The Collingwood supporters, however, were not the type to take such a flogging quietly. As Jackomos recalls, it seemed the only way the Magpies barrackers could respond was through racial abuse, and this abuse towards McAdam and Winmar continued after the game had ended. It was this post-match abuse which led to the statement that made the game so memorable.

6

The gesture
and the photos

*'It was definitely a
racial thing and it's
really important!'*

Saturday 26 September 1970. Collingwood were playing
Carlton in the grand final at the MCG. The scene was set
for the most memorable Australian Rules football image
in decades. Four photographers waited, eager to catch the
pivotal moment of the match. While the *Australian*'s Allan
Funnell was at ground level, three others sat together high
up in the members' grandstand – Dennis Bull from the
Age, Bruce Howard from the *Herald*, and Clive MacKinnon from the *Sun*. It was almost half-time, and Collingwood seemed to have the game in hand, up by 44 points.
With the ball in the Magpies' forward line, Bull decided
to have a mint, offering one to Howard and Mackinnon

at the same time. Out of the corner of his eye, Mackinnon saw David 'Swan' McKay kick the ball high. With a loud yell he dropped his mint and grabbed his camera, Howard and Bull following suit. The three were just in time to see Alex Jesaulenko leap spectacularly over Collingwood ruckman Graeme Jenkin to mark the ball. In those days before fast-snapping shutters, photographers got only one chance. Mackinnon caught the scene just before 'Jezza' marked it, Bull and Howard snapping a frame later, with Funnell capturing it front on from ground level. The mark would later be seen as the game's turning point, and in 2000 it was declared 'the mark of the century'. Yet in a moment of distraction, three key images of the famous mark were almost missed.

Twenty-three years later, on 17 April 1993, all bar two photographers missed an even more famous scene. The TV cameras, assorted media commentators and newspaper journalists were all looking elsewhere when Nicky Winmar made his now-iconic gesture. Perhaps they agreed with the umpires that Gilbert McAdam was best on ground – McAdam later received three Brownlow votes for the game, and Winmar two – and were watching Gilbert as he ran over to the Saints barrackers and shared his delight with them. Wayne Ludbey from the *Sunday Age* and John Feder from the *Sunday Herald-Sun*, however, kept an eye on Winmar as well as McAdam. Both photographers had drowned out the words of the crowd while focusing on the play. But they knew the Collingwood barrackers had given the two Aboriginal players heaps. The antennae both photographers had developed in the last few years meant they knew much of this abuse was racially based. And they sensed that it might be Winmar who would deliver the shot that captured the essence of St Kilda's triumph over Collingwood. As Feder later noted, reflecting on their shared focus on Winmar, 'I think we both prided ourselves on looking for something maybe a bit extra than just the action'.

Camera technology had improved between 1970, when the photographers nearly missed Jezza's famous mark, and 1993. Ludbey and Feder were now shooting in colour, yet there were still no rapid-fire lens shutters. There was only one chance when a memorable shot presented itself. When the moment came, both photographers were ready. As the siren blew, Winmar again found himself near the Magpies cheer squad. Before the baying spectators, he raised his arms in the air and turned around in a circle like a triumphant fighter saluting a hostile crowd. Then he appeared to react as if he'd heard another venomous comment. Turning to face the Collingwood barrackers, Winmar lifted his jumper, pointed to his stomach and said, 'I'm black and I'm proud to be black'. He then blew kisses to the crowd and jogged off to embrace McAdam in a bear hug. The two young sports snappers knew they had amazing shots. Yet both would now have major battles getting their newspaper editors to publish them.

Winmar's gesture was compelling. Like many other key images of the Aboriginal rights movement, it was at once a searing protest and a powerful 'statement of presence' and identity. Yet it also brought something new to the protest images of Indigenous Australians – a clear declaration of pride. Here the link was to the Black Power salute, but its spontaneity lent a more personal tone. Standing tall, Winmar's pose was both intimate and public, a pronouncement of pride in the form of an open challenge. It remains an arresting statement of race, discrimination, dignity and defiance.

The power of Winmar's act was immediately apparent to many of those who witnessed it at the ground that day. The Australian historian and passionate Collingwood fan Joy Damousi can conjure the memory in an instant. For a child of Greek migrants, footy was a place of community and fervour. As she'd grown into adulthood, Damousi had become increasingly uncomfortable with the racist comments of fellow barrackers, yet it was hard to intervene. Still, the vehement barbs thrown at McAdam and Winmar had led to 'discussions and disagreements' in the crowd and 'created a very tense atmosphere'. So 'it came as a relief' when Nicky Winmar 'pulled up his jumper and pointed at his chest' because 'we could all just cheer him in celebration of the message he was trying to send out, and finally silence those racists in the crowd'. Nevertheless, it was a 'very depressing moment' for Damousi, the lowest point in over 40 years of barracking for the Pies, and the beginning of 'a very low point in the club's history'.

Andrew Jackomos remembers being struck by Winmar's 'magnificent physique' as he stood with jersey raised and finger at his torso, the visual poignancy of the stance a fitting and irrefutable rebuke to the racial taunts. Like Damousi, he was gladdened to see a response to the 'disgusting' abuse, especially from someone as impressive as Winmar. The intense, 'high pitched' racist din had reminded him of Wagner's 'Pride of the Valkyries' in the movie *Apocalypse Now* as the helicopters flew over. The sound seared into his memory.

But not all witnesses to Winmar's action understood it at the time. Jess Roberts, a fifteen-year-old third-generation Magpie stalwart, was in the members stand with her father, brother and uncles. She had a close-up view. She knew all the people around her, regulars like her family. One woman was 'madly in love with certain players, so anytime they went near the ball and someone else touched them, that was it; you were written off for the rest of the game and she had a long memory'. There was also one man who 'used to say some awful things', prompting her dad and uncle to warn him to be more civil. 'There were times when my dad and my uncle would say something to him around, you know, "Mate, just ease off a little bit, we all love Collingwood, but let's get …"'

Jess vividly remembers the overall racist abuse that day, but didn't think that it was particularly exceptional or different from other game days. 'There were racial comments that were coming from the crowd, but they weren't any more than usual.' Much of the abuse, she believed, was simply 'pure discrimination against anyone that was not Collingwood'. She also recalls the booing, the tension of the game itself, and the disappointment of the loss and the way Winmar and McAdam 'carved us up'. So when Winmar lifted his jumper, she was confused. 'It didn't make sense to me, it didn't make sense to me at all because … my perspective was purely Collingwood, we've just lost, it's no fun and it came more from that point of view … I could see what he was doing, but I didn't make any connections at the time.' On the day, she recalled that 'it was interesting to see someone that really stood up and had a go back' at her boisterous fellow fans, but she felt then that a gesture of defiant pride would have made more sense coming from McAdam given the number of goals he had scored that day.

Paul Stewart's response was similar to Roberts's. It seemed to him that many in the stands couldn't distinguish between Winmar and McAdam. They were 'both on fire and they were merged into one because of their skin colour' as 'black bastards'. Stewart 'could differentiate between the two' but got the message – separately or together it didn't matter, 'they are actually flogging us'. But he wasn't close enough to realise that Winmar was responding to racial abuse. 'Then I remember him lifting his top up and I thought, "What's he carrying on about?"'

For both Roberts and Stewart, the meaning became apparent later, aided by the publication of the photograph and the discussion that ensued. Not only did the picture help make sense of the moment by allowing for reflection, interpretation and discussion, but it also captured the incident for those who weren't in attendance or who hadn't been looking. Indeed, most of the players missed the moment, focusing instead on their team's defeat or victory. Even Gilbert McAdam didn't learn about Winmar's gesture until he saw the photograph the next day. Fortunately, both Ludbey and Feder had not only seen Winmar's action, but had captured it on film. They also understood something of the gesture's significance. But as each recollects, their editors were not initially convinced that Winmar's statement was that important.

. . . . . .

As soon as he got off the ground, Wayne Ludbey gave Nick Place a call. An old schoolmate from Kingswood College, Place was working as the football editor at the *Sunday Age*. It was his job to follow all the Saturday games, work out what was going to be the biggest football story, and to sort the key statistics and tales from the individual games. The deadline for the first edition of the paper was early Saturday evening, so there was little time to get a coherent sports section after the footy games finished around 5 pm. Place would have been creating an initial mock-up well before then. St Kilda beating Collingwood was already a huge result, the football story of the year so far. But soon Nick Place found that there was more to the game than just the result. 'I still remember Wayne ringing up saying, "Hey, Nicko, I've got an amazing thing here".'

Ludbey had left the game as a man on a mission. As soon as he'd captured Winmar lifting his top and pointing to his skin, Ludbey had started running towards him, snapping busily on his short lens camera. As a result, he was one of the few people to be close enough to hear Nicky Winmar say 'I'm black and I'm proud to be black' as he made his gesture. As he got closer, Ludbey could see that Winmar was clearly upset at being abused all day and racked with intense emotion. Winmar then turned and jogged to embrace Gilbert McAdam, still saying over and over again, 'I'm proud to be black'.

John Feder was further behind Ludbey, shooting with a bigger, 400-millimetre lens. Winmar was perhaps 10 to 15 metres away when the incident occurred. Feder remembers his concentration as he focused the manual camera, shooting at the lowest possible shutter speed because of the darkening sky. His bigger lens meant his picture had Winmar in sharp focus and intensely coloured, shot from the knees up with the background blown out. In contrast, Ludbey had a full-body shot that was more defined at the top and less focused towards the feet due to a damaged lens. ('I have a reputation of being particularly tough on gear', Ludbey observed wryly later.) Unlike Ludbey, Feder didn't hear what Winmar was saying over his whirring camera motor drive and the noise of the crowd. But it was still clear to Feder that Winmar was responding to the racial abuse that had been hurled at him all day. He returned to the *Herald-Sun* offices with a definite understanding of Aboriginal pride and anti-racist sentiments entailed in the gesture. 'That's my main memory with Winmar, knowing it was significant. Very significant', Feder recalls.

When Ludbey arrived back at the *Sunday Age* he quickly had a battle on his hands. Ludbey recalls Ken Merrigan, the sports editor, immediately selected the image of Winmar with his hands in the air for the cover of the Sports section. This left the image of Winmar pointing to his skin, which Ludbey felt clearly belonged on the front page. Yet the *Sunday Age*'s editor, Bruce Guthrie, already had a main, front-page exclusive on Australian paedophiles in Thailand that had been set since midday Friday, a ground-breaking story in itself that would later win a Walkley Award. And the rest of the front page was taken up with breaking news concerning international events related to race. One story focused on new race-riots in South Africa, while another trumpeted the guilty verdict that the civil trial had just passed down on the Los Angeles police officers who had beaten Rodney King.

As Guthrie retells it, the issue was not whether Ludbey's photograph would appear on the front page, but where it would be positioned on that page. But Ludbey clearly remembers initially losing the argument to have the photo appear on the front page. A mere 'snapper', Ludbey felt 'way down there' in the caste system of the newspaper world. It was uncommon for a photographer to battle with his seniors over how an image was used. Ludbey might have been supported by the sports journalists at the game if they had seen Winmar's action, but they hadn't. There was no space on the front page – the layout was ready, the editor happy. Under normal circumstances that would have been it. No further discussion.

But these weren't normal circumstances. Ludbey was driven by a burning sense that 'this is really significant, it's got to be recorded'. He was determined – and a little crazed. 'You had this mad photographer running around saying, "Look, this is a very significant moment, he's raised his jumper, pointing to his skin and saying, I'm proud to be black, in response to racial abuse" – so it'd be – it'd almost be like saying, you know, there's extra-terrestrial life in fucking Collins Street.' Ludbey doesn't think he was 'being noble or anything, I was just doing my job'. Still, it was rare for him or other photographers to stick their neck out like this.

When Ludbey's former schoolmate, Nick Place, joined him in lobbying for the photo, 'one madman became two' as Ludbey put it. As soon as Place saw the picture he 'knew it was an amazing photo'. 'I thought, "Go Winmar, good on you". I knew it was a powerful moment, for someone to have had the courage to say to the racist fans over the fence, "Yeah I'm black and proud of it".' Place knew Wayne Ludbey well. His older sister had been in Ludbey's year at Kingswood and Nick had struck up a friendship with Wayne, the two of them going surfing together. Richard Cotter was still teaching history at Kingswood when Nick Place did his final year. And Cotter was still teaching on the frontier battles that had marked the coming of the British to Australia. 'I was definitely aware of that early Aboriginal history coming out of Kingswood. Of things like Indigenous people being driven off cliffs. I knew there had not been a peaceful white takeover of Australia.' Nick was also training at the Fitzroy Stars Gym and knew lots of the Koori folk who frequented the gym. Nick Place could therefore attest to both Wayne Ludbey's integrity and the importance of Winmar's gesture.

Unlike Ludbey, Place was used to arguing with the editors. 'That was my job, to give my opinion.' Having failed to convince his superiors, Ludbey now sat back and let Nick Place have a go. 'I remember Nick actually went over to the editor and lobbied and then they came to me and said it got in the paper.' It was an eleventh-hour decision, made only about 40 or so minutes before the 8 pm printing deadline that Saturday night. Ludbey recalls that 'I think Bruce came over and he said, "Ease up, we're going to run it'". The photo would get on the front page with an accompanying piece by Place detailing what Ludbey had heard Winmar say. Yet Ludbey assumed this meant his photograph and Place's article would 'knock off' the paedophilia feature story. Instead the picture and story ran as a single column in the very small space reserved for news that had broken at the last minute. Ludbey was disappointed when he saw the size. But he credits Guthrie, a 'terrific editor', for taking a chance. In hindsight, Guthrie's judgment to run both stories was validated – Paul Robinson's paedophilia feature story won a Walkley Award and Ludbey's photograph was a finalist in the category of best coverage of a news story.

The photo and story in the *Sunday Age* on 18 April 1993 might have been small, but the headline grabbed attention. 'Winmar: I'm black and proud of it' it read, above the caption 'Saints and sinners: Nicky Winmar responds to yesterday's racial taunts'. The cover of the paper's Sports section also featured Winmar, but in a very different way. Here, he appeared with his arms raised, beneath the headline 'Saints be Praised'. It was a traditional image of sporting triumph, not racial pride. Ludbey recalls that Merrigan, the sports editor, later wished he had chosen the jumper-raising photograph instead. Ludbey's image of Winmar blowing kisses was not published until the following month and not linked to the on-field protest.

. . . . .

Over at the *Sunday Herald-Sun* offices, John Feder was also arguing with his editors. First there was a struggle to get the image on the front page. The editor, Ian Moore, was from Sydney, and deputy editor Lyall Corless remembers that Moore took some convincing that the image was important enough to get it on the front page. Moore eventually agreed, and it became the main front-page photograph. But Feder's strongest memory of the incident is the discussion he had with Corless and sports editor Scot Palmer over what Winmar had said. 'I remember the argument clearly. I can remember doing the photocopy of the picture and having the argument there'. The editors were arguing that 'Winmar was saying, "Look at me, I've got guts"' while Feder was saying, 'No, no, no, he was pointing to the colour of his skin, it was definitely a racial thing and it's really important!'

Like with Wayne Ludbey, it was unusual for Feder to argue with his superiors. He was normally happy to leave the editors to decide how to use his pictures. 'I wouldn't argue with them often, but I felt strongly about the picture and the moment.' Nonetheless, he regularly filled in for the paper's picture editor, and felt comfortable having vigorous discussions with the paper's senior staff. Feder was surprised that his paper wasn't making 'a big enough deal of it'. He feels they 'begrudgingly put it on the front', but refused to refer to racism in the caption to the picture because they remained wary of the racial element of Winmar's gesture.

The first edition of the *Sunday Herald-Sun* captioned the image, 'Nicky Winmar answers the Collingwood taunts'. It ignored race and interpreted Winmar's message to be 'How good am I?' after he 'copped plenty of flak' from the Collingwood supporters. The later edition recaptioned the photo, declaring Winmar's message to be 'We won with determination'. These captions seem bizarre in light of what the image is now famous for. Perhaps the paper was simply ignoring the issue of racist taunts, as the *Sunday Herald-Sun* journalist Neil Roberts advised the Indigenous player Chris Lewis to do in the sports pages that very weekend. Or perhaps the editors genuinely did not realise the significance of Winmar's gesture and words. For John Feder it was an indication that 'these issues weren't seen as that important, or as important as they should be'.

. . . . . .

When Nick Place saw the *Sunday Herald-Sun* interpretation 'How good am I?', he laughed. 'Wow', he thought, 'really, that's what you're going with?' Still, he himself had been placed in the awkward position of writing what would become a key story about an event that he hadn't witnessed. The truth was neither Place nor anyone else involved in the publication of the image knew how important it was going to be. Just how vital it would be 'to blackfellas standing up', as Place later put it. A few weeks later, Place was away holidaying by the Murray River on a long weekend when he got a call from his sister. Also a journalist, she told him that he'd just featured on ABC TV's 'Media Watch'. 'Oh no', Nick thought, 'what have I done?' But the 'Media Watch' story celebrated Ludbey and Place as heroes, condemning the captions used by the *Herald-Sun*. Would the story 'ever have come to light', presenter Stuart Littlemore asked, 'if photographer Ludbey hadn't passed on the words to go with his picture'?

The 'Media Watch' story was testament to the importance that the image of Nicky Winmar pointing to his skin had already come to hold. Wayne Ludbey remembers having people call him up a number of times to check his story but didn't hear them identify which media organisation they were with. When Ludbey saw the discussions he'd had with these people quoted on 'Media Watch', he thought, 'you pricks!' But in the end he was glad 'Media Watch' had done it, for Ludbey was carrying the burden of being the only person to publicly report what Winmar had said.

Pictures may tell a thousand words, but the captions that seek to explain, and in this case possibly corral them, are vital. In the years following the publication of the two Nicky Winmar images, a story took hold that Winmar had simply been saying that 'he had guts'. The story continues to circulate, despite Wayne Ludbey's eyewitness account and Winmar's repeated confirmation that he stated he was proud to be black. It is as if some people want to undercut the power of the image by arguing that it was not a compelling response to racist abuse. Perhaps it reflects a discomfort at the response the image provoked and the iconic place the two photographs have come to hold. In time the publication of the images of Winmar's gesture would lay bare much of Australia's problematic race relations and come to symbolise the call for change.

7

The response

'As long as they conduct themselves like white people'

Reactions to the photos of Nicky Winmar were immediate and intense. For many Indigenous Australians the importance of the gesture was instantly apparent. Caroline Martin remembers being spellbound when she opened the Sunday papers – she'd never seen such a powerful image. 'It actually gave us a voice and said, "We are strong and we are proud.".' As Gilbert McAdam noted, it 'reinforced that our people around Australia are proud of who we are and how far we've come'. 'Wow', a stunned McAdam had thought when he'd first seen the picture, 'where was I?' McAdam's only regret was that he hadn't seen Nicky's gesture and joined him – sharing the iconic moment like Tommie Smith and John Carlos shared their Black Power salute in 1968.

Other Australians were also inspired by the gesture. Lawyer, scholar and journalist Waleed Aly was fourteen at the time, and dealing with life in Melbourne as a dark-skinned son of Egyptian parents. When Aly saw the image and read Winmar's declaration that he was black and proud of it, it was like an epiphany. 'The immediate thought that came to me was: "So am I!" … Until then I hadn't been given permission by a public role model to have that thought. I was able at that moment to look out to a football field and see the possibility of a projection of myself. I can't really convey how important that is, I think, particularly for kids to grow up and be able to see that.'

Many recognised the image as a vital call for change. The most prominent of these was Senator Nick Bolkus, then minister for Immigration and Ethnic Affairs. Senator Bolkus was in Sydney on the day the image was published, preparing to open a United Nations conference on racism that Australia was hosting. Some might have been embarrassed to have Australia's flawed race relations revealed so publicly on the eve of the conference, but Bolkus embraced the moment, celebrating Winmar's action and words. Australia, noted Bolkus, was an 'unsettled nation' struggling with widespread racism that needed to be eliminated before a 'fully Australian identity' could be developed. By declaring himself proud to be black, Nicky Winmar 'stood for the way ahead in Australia', with Australians having a responsibility to 'tear down' racial barriers. Yet while Bolkus was upbeat, he also cautioned that the abuse which had led to Winmar's gesture 'reflected badly on our society'. And Bolkus also called on the AFL to 'act aggressively to wipe out such racism'.

Winmar himself felt excited that his gesture might lead to change. 'Yes!' he exclaimed when he saw the photos, glad that finally it seemed like 'there is someone out there that is thinking like I'm thinking, just give us a chance'. The first response of the AFL, however, was defensive. They wanted to avoid a controversy rather than focus on their failings. The AFL Commission stated that they 'abhorred racism' but at the same time did not believe any changes in rules or processes were necessary.

Nor did St Kilda want to be distracted. The victory against Collingwood at Victoria Park showed that they were on the right track after decades of disappointment. Like the West Coast Eagles of 1991, the Saints hoped to steer clear of a debate over race. So St Kilda emphasised their complete disagreement 'with anything remotely racist' while at the same time forbidding Winmar and McAdam from speaking to the media. It says much about the attitudes and understandings of the time that this 'silencing' of the key players was noted only in passing.

Gilbert McAdam felt like St Kilda was trying to protect him and Winmar from the media circus and to help them focus on the coming game against Carlton. But later he wondered if things might have moved more quickly if he and Winmar had been able to discuss the vilification they were constantly receiving from opposition players and supporters. Still, the world of football chewed up those who couldn't turn their full attention to the coming week, so McAdam tried to put the issue to the side and began preparing for Carlton.

The *Herald-Sun* was also careful not to fan the flames of any controversy over racism in footy. In line with their captioning of John Feder's photo, the paper chose initially to ignore the issue. Over the next week no mention was made of Winmar's gesture and the growing response to it. Already disappointed by the captions, Feder could do little but move on to the next week's games.

Wayne Ludbey, however, was beset by conflicting emotions. He'd done his job, ensuring that an amazing act of courage was properly reported and recognised. He felt inspired by what Winmar had done. Yet Ludbey had also put his credibility on the line – people only knew Winmar had declared his pride in being black because Ludbey had heard it and made sure those comments were published. Already some people were questioning his motives, with a few even directing abuse at him. 'Nigger in the woodpile' was one such comment, referring to his curly hair and tanned skin.

As the debate and reactions escalated, the loneliness of Ludbey's position began to weigh on him. And so, not knowing that Winmar had been gagged, Ludbey drove out to the Saints ground after training on the Wednesday. He wanted to tell Nicky 'how incredibly courageous' his gesture had been, to give him some big prints of the image, and to chat with Winmar about what he had said. The shy Winmar, however, wasn't allowed to speak to the media, and so only smiled and said thanks. Ludbey felt more exposed than ever. He could draw some solace, though, from the way his paper, the *Age*, was leading the calls for change.

. . . . . .

Discussing racial abuse in footy had long been taboo. And while Essendon and Syd Jackson had sought to open up discussion and bring about solutions, it was Winmar's gesture that brought the first widespread response to this racial vilification. As *Sydney Morning Herald* journalist Gerard Wright noted in his match report on the Monday after the game, 'The sub-text to this is that there is in Melbourne a slowly rising groundswell against the racism that has been part of the game for the past 25 years'. The problem, as Wright noted, was how to respond. Michael Long had replied with his fists and been suspended. Syd Jackson wanted a 'code of conduct' in consultation with the Human Rights Commission, but until then advocated 'turning the other cheek'. Now Winmar had found a way of unmasking the racism with a striking gesture of pride. Like many others, Wright was full of praise for Winmar. 'As spectacularly talented as he is with or near a football, Winmar has never been more eloquent or effective for his cause or his colour than he was in that moment.'

Wright's article was complemented by a front-page column from senior sports journalist Garry Linnell, who decried football's disconnect with Australia's values. 'We pride ourselves on living in a supposedly enlightened society, one where most people strive for equality. Yet football remains curiously apart.' Linnell accused football and other Australian sports of 'subtly' condoning racism by celebrating those who do 'anything to gain the advantage over an opponent'. Winmar had responded to the abuse of people whom Linnell caustically referred to as 'neanderthals', 'brain-damaged' and 'moronic'. But Linnell thought it was more realistic for the AFL to stamp out racism on the field first by making racial abuse a reportable offence. 'Let's see some of these players called before the tribunal and asked to publicly justify their use of racist taunts.'

By Tuesday the *Age* was demanding action from the AFL. 'There is no place for racism in football and the AFL must do everything in its power to make sure its players – and, if possible, spectators – understand this', thundered the editorial. The AFL weakly argued that on-field vilification was already reportable under a provision dealing with 'a player who uses abusive, threatening or insulting language'. Yet as Patrick Smith – another senior *Age* sports journalist – observed, 'no player has been reported, let alone punished for racist remarks'. He wanted the AFL to go further and 'specify that racist remarks from one player to another constitutes abuse that is outside the laws of the game'. It was time for the AFL to do its bit against the scourge of racism. 'By outlawing racism, the AFL would be signalling to the public at large that this kind of ugly behaviour is unacceptable on either side of the fence.'

Next to the *Age* editorial was a cartoon of the incident by Peter Nicholson. In this brilliant drawing, later nominated for best cartoon in the 1993 Walkley Awards, Nicholson depicted Winmar facing the baying Collingwood spectators. A proud, athletic and dignified Winmar was mirrored by an obese, rabid, hate-filled barracker lifting his top to expose his fat white gut, bringing to mind the racist 'neanderthals', 'brain-damaged' and 'moronic spectators' bagged by Garry Linnell in the *Age* the previous day.

Eighteen months earlier Caroline Wilson had spoken out about the racial abuse entrenched in footy's culture. Racism was becoming a detested word in Australian society and yet was seemingly on the increase in football circles. Collingwood captain Tony Shaw's brutally honest statement that he'd 'make a racist comment every week if it would help win the game' had caused a stir, and then been forgotten. But not everything remains forgotten. On the Tuesday after Winmar's gesture, Patrick Smith reprinted Shaw's quote. This time the words had a lasting impact.

. . . . . .

Collingwood were under fire. Nicky Winmar and Gilbert McAdam might have been gagged, the *Herald-Sun* silent, but it still felt to Joy Damousi that everyone she bumped into wanted to talk about Winmar's gesture. Most of Melbourne seemed horrified by the abuse howled that day by Magpies supporters. Damousi shared their horror and felt ashamed by the club that represented her, the club she loved. It was the 'lowest point' in her time following the Magpies, and Damousi took the most drastic step she could think of. She stopped attending games and cancelled her membership of the club.

Damousi was by no means alone. Bill Murnane wrote to the *Age* that as 'a Collingwood fan, I am profoundly disturbed to learn that our captain believes racial abuse is a legitimate weapon on the field ... If this cannot be retracted by Shaw and the club, I have attended my last game for Collingwood'. Gaylene Seadon penned a similar letter, noting that while she was a 'Collingwood supporter' she 'certainly didn't support racism on the ground or off field'. 'Tony Shaw', Gaylene suggested, 'should spend more time with the Aboriginal community'.

Those who didn't follow Collingwood were also quick to contact the *Age* and *Herald-Sun*. All shared a similar theme. The Magpies were condemned while Winmar and McAdam were applauded. 'Bravo to Nicky Winmar for his comment on racism', wrote Kieran Carrell, who had been 'horrified to hear the abuse around me directed at Winmar and co' in a game at Victoria Park in 1990. 'Midnite' from Keon Park was more forthright. 'I write to vent my disgust at those Collingwood supporters, hopefully a minority element, who used such vile, disgusting, racial remarks and abuse to Winmar and McAdam … To Winmar and McAdam I say, well done, stand tall and proud.' These sentiments were echoed by 'M Gillard' for whom Winmar was 'a champion' who stood 'head and shoulders above the morons in the Victoria Park crowd'.

Yet many of the so-called morons felt they were being unfairly targeted. Shouting out abuse was just part of footy, supporters of all clubs groups did it, and the players should be able to cope with it. Or so many Collingwood barrackers argued. Indeed, the *Age* was inundated with calls from 'furious' Pies fans declaiming the paper's 'anti-Collingwood bias'. To a certain extent these supporters had a point. As reporters from both the *Age* and *Herald-Sun* discovered the weekend after Winmar's gesture, fans of all teams seemed to routinely yell out racist abuse. (Notably, the *Herald-Sun* reporters were from the paper's 'news' department — the sport pages were still in ostrich mode.) One 74-year-old woman and long-time Western Bulldogs football supporter, Mary Millard, was happy to confess, 'Of course I sing out "black bastard", but I don't mean it. It's all part of being at the footy on a Saturday arvo'. Such supporters were in

agreement with Allan McAlister, the Collingwood president, who'd dismissed the racist abuse as just 'ballyhoo'
because 'no one is fair dinkum'. Even the *Age*'s columnist
Simon Madden, the former Essendon ruckman and team-
mate of Michael Long, argued that racist sledging was simply part of the game. 'The question for the footballer is not
how to stop [the abuse] but how do you handle it?'

It was as if racial abuse was a trivial matter – a collection of harmless insults that were meant to distract, not
offend, and should be handled as such. What was missing
in these comments was any awareness of damaging assumptions embedded in the insults and of the very real effects of
these assumptions. Soon, however, Allan McAlister would
unwittingly reveal the ugly sentiments that shaped the culture of racist abuse.

. . . . . .

On Sunday 25 April 1993, Allan McAlister walked into
the studios of Channel Nine's 'World of Sports' program. Collingwood had a bye but the talk all week had been
about the racism of its supporters and players, headlined
by the comments of its captain, Tony Shaw. The Collingwood president wanted to defend his club and end the controversy. What he said, though, only escalated the matter.
McAlister tried to assure viewers that the Magpies did not
have an issue with Indigenous Australians, but then add-

ed the following proviso. 'As long as they conduct themselves like white people, well, off the field, everyone will
admire and respect them.' When asked to explain what he
meant, McAlister made his position even clearer. 'As long
as they conduct themselves like human beings, they will be
all right. That's the key.'

McAlister didn't mean to be offensive. But here he was
in 1993 implying that Indigenous Australians were inferi-
or – sub-human even – and could only be redeemed if they
modelled their behaviour on white people. It was an attitude that reflected the racial science of people like Baldwin Spencer – an attitude that had led supposedly civilised
white people to annex the land of Indigenous Australians,
then take their 'mixed race' children away in an attempt
to save them, while also creating appalling segregated living conditions like those Nicky Winmar grew up in. And it
was this attitude that informed the regular verbal abuse of
Indigenous footy players, where the term 'black' was somehow hurled as a grave insult – as if there was something
wrong in being descended from the people who had lived
on this continent for thousands of years.

. . . . . .

Broadcast that evening on TV news bulletins around
Australia, McAlister's comments caused an uproar.
Not surprisingly, the strongest responses came from those

who knew just how damaging notions of white superiority were. Syd Jackson condemned the condescending nature of McAlister's remarks. Robert Nicholls, president of the Aborigines Advancement League and nephew of Sir Douglas Nicholls, demanded McAlister's resignation and called on the AFL to immediately take action to prevent future racial abuse in the sport. And Moira Rayner, Victoria's Equal Opportunity Commissioner and herself a Collingwood supporter, urged the AFL to 'grab the high moral ground' by bringing in measures that made players and spectators alike realise that racism was unacceptable.

Instead of defusing the issue, McAlister's comments had shown exactly why Nicky Winmar had pointed with pride to his skin. And in the ensuing weeks the image of Winmar's gesture was shown over and over again. In one of the most striking depictions, the Sydney cartoonist Rocco Fazzari sketched Winmar against the background of an Aboriginal flag which doubled as a bull's eye. Most poignantly, Fazzari drew the face of an elderly Aboriginal man on Winmar's stomach – eyes closed, perhaps in sorrow – emphasising the heritage in which Winmar was stating his pride. The associated article placed the abuse shouted at Winmar and McAdam alongside several other recent examples of racism towards Indigenous Australians.

McAlister was reviled for his comments, but the resultant furore led to the first moments of change. McAlister himself apologised to Robert Nicholls the next day, then announced that Collingwood players and supporters would be told racism was unacceptable. On the same day Tony Shaw apologised for any on-field remarks 'that caused people to think I was a racist'. Footscray also asked its supporters to refrain from racist abuse, while the AFL announced it would develop a 'code of conduct' for players and club officials, along with an education program for supporters.

McAlister seemed keen to make amends, and in mid-May he flew to the Northern Territory to speak at the Darwin Press Club and apologise again for his remarks. It was a courageous move that was celebrated by the mainstream media. Yet it again revealed problematic assumptions. Collingwood had the biggest Indigenous supporter base of the Melbourne AFL clubs. Though McAlister had met with Robert Nicholls, he had not reached out to the Victorian Indigenous community or attempted to talk with the many local Kooris who followed the Magpies. Instead he was travelling north to apologise, as if that was where the 'real' Aboriginal people lived. As Caroline Martin later noted, 'what Allan McAlister did was make us look invisible. Rather than actually remedy it here, he flew to Melville Island, flew to Darwin and wanted to apologise to the Aboriginal community. It was an act that fed into all the stereotypes of where the Aboriginal communities are'.

The three-day 'goodwill' tour was something of a 'circus'. Crowds of media and locals followed McAlister's every move. He was trying to say the right things, explaining that he didn't 'realise the deepness of the hurt of a simple statement like that ... There's no place for that sort of thing'. And he spoke of organising a biennial Collingwood–Aboriginal All-Star game in Darwin, and lobbying the AFL to recognise Aboriginal contributions to football as part of the 1993 Grand Final.

Still, McAlister's reception was mixed. He spent time with Maurice Rioli, the great Richmond footballer who was now a member of the Northern Territory Parliament. He kicked a footy with kids, handed out Collingwood jumpers and footballs, and put a $100 tab on a bar he visited one afternoon. Yet he was also cursed by one local man who famously pointed a bone at him, and he was initially banned from visiting Melville Island by the Tiwi Land Council. After some intense negotiation McAlister was allowed to visit the island to attend a national Aboriginal sports conference. Here he again apologised, but his apology was boycotted by the Victorian delegates who remained dismayed by McAlister's failure to try and reconcile with the Indigenous Australians in his own backyard. Caroline Martin was one of these delegates and remembers that the protest 'made our mob back home proud'. The mainstream media didn't understand the protest and so dismissed it. Nevertheless, it was another sign that all was not well in Collingwood's relationship with Australia's Indigenous peoples.

. . . . . .

Meanwhile, the AFL season was continuing apace, and not in a happy way for St Kilda. In the week that followed his gesture, Nicky Winmar became embroiled in a contract dispute with the club that led him to miss the next two games. With Tony Lockett and Robert Harvey out injured, the Saints were overrun by Carlton after leading at half-time. Lockett returned for the next game, but that was not enough to beat Richmond. Even with Harvey and Winmar back in the side the team struggled, losing their next three games to end May on a streak of five losses. In contrast Collingwood seemed galvanised after their loss to St Kilda and the controversy that followed. They beat Carlton before accounting for Adelaide and Hawthorn and by late May they had the best record in the AFL. A loss to Fitzroy set the scene for a top-of-the-table clash with North Melbourne. Held on Sunday 31 May at Victoria Park, it was to be another defining moment in the season.

Gilbert McAdam's younger brother Adrian had debuted for North Melbourne earlier in the season with three remarkable games in which he kicked a total of 23 goals. Aware of the reputation of the Collingwood crowd, the North Melbourne cheer squad unfurled a large Aboriginal flag before the game to signal their support for McAdam. Adrian was delighted. 'I saw the flag among our cheer squad, and I felt really good, I knew it was there for me.'

Despite the swirling controversy over racial abuse, members of the Collingwood crowd hurled racist insults at Adrian McAdam throughout the day. 'There was plenty of it', noted Adrian after the game, '"black cunt", "go and sniff on your petrol", you know, heaps of words'. But as with his brother and Nicky Winmar, the foul torrent only increased Adrian's motivation. 'The more the Collingwood crowd called out racist comments, the more I got pumped up.' He dominated the game, kicking nine goals against six different opponents. North Melbourne won easily, smashing Collingwood by 83 points. And late in the game Adrian decided to give a message back to the Magpie faithful, waving mockingly towards the Collingwood outer after his team-mate Wayne Carey kicked a goal in the last quarter.

Once again racist abuse had Collingwood on the front pages of Melbourne's papers. Yet despite Allan McAlister's earlier declaration that Magpies supporters would be urged to refrain from racist remarks, he refused to condemn the abuse of Adrian McAdam. 'We're not entering into that', he stated in response to questions, 'we've had enough'. It was a similar situation in June when the West Coast Eagles played Collingwood at Victoria Park. The Eagles' three Indigenous stars, Chris Lewis, Peter Matera and Troy Ugle, made a pact before the game that they too would rise to another level in the face of the abuse they knew was coming. After Collingwood started brightly, West Coast gradually pegged them back, willed over the line in part by Lewis, Matera and

Ugle. Wayne Ludbey was there to photograph the three of them, arm in arm, after the game – a picture that the *Sunday Age* used on the cover of their sports section the next day. But despite West Coast commenting on the racial abuse directed at their players, Collingwood officials were again largely silent.

It still seemed that the Magpies had 'had enough' of the controversy over racism in footy. But the lack of leadership on the issue meant that some barrackers had had enough of Collingwood. Paul Stewart and his father were so 'pissed off' that they stopped following the club until McAlister and Shaw left. For Paul, Collingwood prided itself on being an 'army', and yet here were the leaders of the army allowing a culture that denigrated the heritage of many Magpie supporters on a regular basis. Paul's mate Anthony McGregor had been drafted by Fitzroy in the lead-up to the 1993 season, and so Paul and his father began to follow the Lions. They missed the tribalism, but how can you be part of a collective where the members don't protect each other?

. . . . . .

The second half of the 1993 season was a case of 'almost' for St Kilda. They won seven of their eleven matches, but couldn't recover the ground they had lost after the Collingwood game and missed the finals by two wins. Collingwood were even more haunted by questions of 'what if?' One of the pre-season favourites, they finished the season just one game out of the top six. Of their nine games at Victoria Park, they had only lost to St Kilda, North Melbourne and the West Coast Eagles – losses that arguably cost them a chance to play in the finals.

Each of these games had been marked by a controversy over racial abuse, yet at least some elements within Collingwood were unrepentant. Speaking on the eve of the finals, star Magpies player Mick McGuane defended the way he and other players said things on the field to Indigenous players that 'you normally wouldn't say if you saw them in the street … You're out there to compete, you're out there to win and do the best for your club, and whatever you say, it might be detrimental at that point of time, but you're doing it for a purpose'. Earlier in the season Allan McAlister had suggested that Collingwood might penalise players who continued to racially abuse opponents. Yet now at the end of the season, McGuane was happy to admit that he'd 'had a go at the Longs, the Kicketts, the Lewises' because they 'pose problems for us if they're very good'. The aim was to enrage them. 'You try to use that to your advantage if you can. If they become sucked in and want to belt you, well beautiful, suits me. Doesn't worry me in the slightest. Then you know you've got 'em. They're off their game, they're not concentrating and they can't play with their natural flair and their natural ability, and that suits me fine.'

These were dispiriting if honest comments, and raised the question of whether anything had changed since 1991 when Tony Shaw gave a similarly honest answer to Caroline Wilson's question about racial abuse in footy. But behind the scenes some things were changing. In July the AFL had appointed Gilbert McAdam as their inaugural Indigenous liaison officer to improve communications with Indigenous players and to help develop the code of conduct. The position was co-funded by the Commonwealth Government after prime minister Paul Keating had suggested that the AFL work to mark 1993 as the International Year of the World's Indigenous People. And with McAdam's help, together with the workings of fate, the 1993 Grand Final week turned into a true celebration of Australia's Indigenous peoples.

. . . . . .

From the perspective of the Essendon Football Club, the 1993 regular season was something of a fairytale. The season had started off in difficult fashion with Michael Long suspended for hitting West Coast captain John Worsfold – an incident which had led Essendon president David Shaw to speak out about the endemic culture of racism in footy. After five rounds the Bombers were struggling with only one win and a draw for their efforts. But they won their next five games to climb back into contention. Their second half of the year was even more impressive, as they won seven of their last nine games to finish on top of the ladder. While they had a number of impressive veterans like Tim Watson, Mark Thompson and Mark Harvey, the footy world was abuzz at the exciting play of Essendon young-sters like Gavin Wanganeen, James Hird, Dustin Fletcher, Mark Mercuri and Joe Misiti, along with that of Michael Long, who had become a force to be reckoned with during the second half of the season.

Dubbed the 'Baby Bombers', their first final was against the second-placed Carlton, a perennial powerhouse. In an intense encounter Essendon looked likely to run away with the match after half-time, only for the Blues captain Ste-phen Kernahan to will Carlton back into the game and lead them to a 2-point victory. Essendon then accounted for West Coast before falling behind to Adelaide in the prelim-inary final. Adelaide were in the midst of their own fairy-tale, having only entered the competition that year. Up by 42 points at half-time, it seemed like the Crows were going to the grand final in their first season. But then the dream turned into a nightmare as Adelaide started to play con-servatively, hoping not to lose, while Essendon ran and ran. When the final siren sounded Essendon had completed an epic comeback to win by 11 points and progress to a grand final where they would meet Carlton once again.

Grand final week began, as always, with the Brown-low Medal count on Monday night. In a surprise result,

Essendon's young Indigenous star Gavin Wanganeen won the medal over Carlton champion Greg Williams. He was the first Indigenous Australian to win the AFL's highest individual award, and couldn't believe the honour. Wayne Ludbey was one of the photographers travelling in the car with Wanganeen after the Brownlow count ended, and he remembers Wanganeen proudly and delightedly murmuring to himself that he was the first Nunga (Indigenous South Australian) to win the medal. Gilbert McAdam and the AFL couldn't have scripted it better as they prepared for a grand final that would celebrate Australia's Indigenous peoples. And the fantasy scripting continued.

In the International Year of the World's Indigenous People, the AFL's grand final poster and *Football Record* cover was an evocative painting of two footballers, one black and the other white, flying for the ball set on a background of an oval with people of all colours streaming inside, all represented in dots like a bark painting. The grand final entertainment began with a performance by renowned Aboriginal opera singer Maroochy Barambah, who also sang the national anthem. Then at half-time an eerie, evocative didgeridoo solo reverberated around the ground, played by Gunnai man Wayne Thorpe who sat atop the main scoreboard, followed by a performance from Yothu Yindi who had members of the crowd dancing in the stands to their hit song 'Treaty'.

By now the grand final was already in the control of

Essendon who were leading by 37 points. In just the second minute Michael Long had given a glimpse of what was to come – after receiving the ball in the middle of the ground he sped past opponents, running for 75 metres to kick the goal of the match. So fast, elusive and skilful was Long that later in the game the Carlton players started trying to corral him to prevent his run. It didn't work. Long waited patiently for the attempted tackle that never came, then dashed past the despairing defenders anyway. As the game came to an end Long once more sliced through the middle before passing to Gavin Wanganeen who kicked the final goal of the game.

Clearly best on ground, Michael Long was duly awarded the Norm Smith Medal which was presented by the only other Indigenous player to have won it, Maurice Rioli. After a season that had begun with the ignominy of abuse and another suspension for Long, the shy Tiwi Islander was now calm, confident and happy to talk. In post-match interviews, Long spoke about the thrill of winning the premiership and how he'd dreamed of accomplishing this in the International Year of the World's Indigenous People. He also spoke for the first time about the racism he'd experienced, and his belief that education would eliminate the scourge. For Indigenous Australians, it was an amazing end to a turbulent year, and the future looked bright. But other, untold, stories showed that there was still significant resistance to change.

O n 3 November 1993, Gavin Wanganeen received a further honour – the award of National Sportsman of the Year at the fourth National Aboriginal and Torres Strait Islander Sports Awards. The ceremony was held in Melbourne, and had been promoted via a poster depicting Nicky Winmar pointing with pride to his skin. The poster was the idea of Andrew Jackomos, who'd organised the event in his capacity as the Victorian manager of the Aboriginal and Torres Strait Islander Commission (ATSIC). Though it was almost seven months later, Jackomos still had vivid memories of Winmar gesturing strikingly in front of him and the other Magpies social club members, celebrating his heritage and the colour of his skin. Jackomos was still inspired by the gesture, as were many other Indigenous Australians. Indeed, many of those at the dinner would take their own copies of the poster back with them and have it framed. Yet the response of Jackomos's footy club, Collingwood, still rankled.

Back in April, Jackomos had written a letter to the Magpies offering his services to help educate staff and players around the issue of racism. He explained that he was a long-time social club member who worked for ATSIC. Yet not only did Jackomos never hear back from the club he never received a renewal notice for his 1994 social club membership, nor did his friend who had written a similar letter. When Jackomos phoned the club to let them know he had not received his renewal notice, they promised to send it out and that someone would call him back. Neither letter nor call eventuated despite repeated contact. In the end Jackomos was left to assume that his offer to help improve the culture of Collingwood had led them to cancel his membership. It was a stark refutation of Collingwood's stated commitment to abolishing racism in footy, and a sign that despite the impact of Nicky Winmar's gesture, the optimism of Michael Long and others would soon be sorely tested.

8

The next step

*'I've had enough
of this shit. I don't
have to take it.'*

Wayne Ludbey had never seen Michael Long so mad. He
looked 'fucking furious'. It was 5 May 1995, and Ludbey
was one of the many media figures gathered at the MCG
for an AFL press conference concerning the latest incident
of racial abuse. Long had formally complained that Collingwood's ruck, Damian Monkhorst, had racially abused him
during the Anzac Day match on 25 April 1995. Long and
Monkhorst were at the press conference, yet neither spoke.
Instead AFL chief executive officer, Ross Oakley, did all the
talking. Standing between Long and Monkhorst, Oakley
announced that the matter had been resolved to everyone's
satisfaction, and with the issue now behind them, the two
players were just keen to get back to playing footy.

Oakley was wrong. Michael Long was clearly anything but satisfied. Indeed, Ludbey could tell that 'as soon as Michael walked in he wasn't happy'. As Oakley spoke, Ludbey saw Long becoming 'more and more agitated'. The jarring red of the Coke advertisement behind Long seemed strangely apt as his anger mounted. But looking straight ahead at the media contingent, Oakley seemed unaware of Long's distress. Using sign language, Long signalled to the bemused journalists, photographers and camera crews that he'd been gagged. Ludbey recalls him gesturing with his finger, mimicking slicing his throat.

It was the beginning of the next key step in the fight against racism in Australian Rules football – a fight that would lead to ground-breaking laws against racial abuse. Wayne Ludbey now worked for the *Herald Sun*, and his picture of Oakley, Monkhorst and the furious Long featured on the cover of the newspaper the next day beneath the large headline, 'GAGGED'. Yet unlike the shot of Winmar that Ludbey and Feder had captured in 1993, the photo of the press conference failed to fully convey the drama and tension of the moment. Nor could it so perfectly signal the issues at stake. Without such an expressive image, journalists and other commentators returned repeatedly to the poignant Winmar photograph. And while Michael Long now led the fight against racism, Nicky Winmar's actions continued to symbolise the pride, defiance and demand for change at the heart of this battle.

. . . . . .

Michael Long had ended the 1993 season on a high. He'd been best on ground in the grand final, helping secure Essendon a premiership in the International Year of the World's Indigenous People. And while he was still on the receiving end of racist insults and taunts, along with the occasional offensive letter, it seemed like positive change was on the way. The AFL had responded to the furore over Winmar's gesture and Allan McAlister's comments by pledging to eradicate racism in footy, and Long hoped that their actions, together with education, would resolve the problem.

For a time the promise held. Gilbert McAdam had moved to the Brisbane Bears for the 1994 season in order to be closer to his wife's family, but he continued his work as the AFL's Indigenous liaison officer. In 1994 McAdam helped organise a pre-season Aboriginal All-Stars game in Darwin. Their opponent was Collingwood, with Magpies president Allan McAlister making good on his commitment to help re-establish the concept after the first such All-Stars game in 1983. Prime minister Paul Keating expressed hoped that the AFL's 'reconciliation game' might help bring about a sense of national unity.

Flying to Darwin in order to watch the match, the prime minister (and Collingwood supporter) hoped to use the attention generated by the contest to reshape the continuing debate over the High Court's Mabo decision. On the eve of the match Keating drew on sporting metaphors of 'a fair go' and 'support for the underdog' to urge Australians to 'work with a common national purpose' and reject racist abuse that was 'abhorrent to our best tradition and the best tradition of sport'. Keating also expressed optimism that the 'tide had turned', adding that 'I truly believe the game has changed between black and white Australia'.

Keating's presence at the game was a testament to the way Nicky Winmar's gesture had started a national conversation about racism. As Daniel Lewis of the *Sydney Morning Herald* noted, 'For millions of sports-obsessed Australians, it is likely that the actions of one man on a football field in 1993 did more to raise awareness of Aboriginality and racism than the International Year of the World's Indigenous People, [Mr M] Yunupingu being named Australian of the Year or the Mabo legislation'. Yet, although selected in the All-Star team, Winmar wasn't in Darwin. St Kilda had denied him clearance, arguing that they couldn't afford for their star to take time off from pre-season training to play in the game. Perhaps the Saints also remained wary of the controversy over racism. If so, they only succeeded in creating a further media storm. The decision was roundly condemned, with high-profile figures like Robert Tickner, the minister for Aboriginal and Torres Strait Islander Affairs, lamenting Winmar's absence from a game that 'has the potential to amount to a very significant step in the reconciliation process'. St Kilda, however, stood firm, with football manager Gary Colling reportedly observing 'that even a phone call from Paul Keating' wouldn't change his mind.

In a contest rich with symbolic meaning, the All-Stars triumphed over Collingwood by 20 points. 'For 100 Minutes, Racism Is Defeated', proclaimed the front page of the *Sunday Age*. Collingwood was gracious in defeat, with Magpie officials seeking closure. 'I think any person who yells a racist comment over the fence is going to be looked at very nastily', stated Collingwood coach Leigh Matthews after the match. 'If it was a problem, I don't think it's going to be a problem in the future.' All-Stars captain Michael McLean shared the hope that the game had 'helped educate young people about racism'. Yet once again comments by Allan McAlister gave reason to temper optimism.

Promoting the contest as a chance to 'knock racism on the head', McAlister nevertheless claimed that on-field taunts about colour and heritage were 'not racism, they're tactics'. 'You'll never stop the remarks of one player to another to try and get an edge on him', McAlister explained. 'That's what it's all about, they're big men, they're big boys, they know what it's all about.' Extraordinarily, what made it all okay in McAlister's mind, indeed 'the real plus', was 'the moment they finish and get off the field it's all forgotten' by the Indigenous players. 'They're not interested.'

It was another remarkably revealing statement by someone trying not to offend. However, this time McAlister withdrew his comments almost immediately, adding in response to a question that racial remarks were not okay 'anywhere'. The quick retraction coupled with the arrival of the prime minister overshadowed McAlister's slip and it was quickly forgotten. Yet his comments highlighted the entrenched belief that what happened on the field – in the heat of the game – stayed on the field and had no consequences off it. And it was this attitude that Michael Long and other Indigenous players would battle.

. . . . . .

As Aboriginal liaison officer, Gilbert McAdam attended Under 18s carnivals, speaking to young Aboriginal players about racism. 'We were telling the younger ones that when they get in the system not to put up with it.' In 1994, Che Cockatoo-Collins, one of the new generation of Indigenous players, debuted for Essendon as a 17-year-old. Cockatoo-Collins wasn't prepared to be silent about the racist taunts that he received over the course of the first few months of his AFL career, but raising it publicly didn't seem to help. As he reflected a year later at the beginning of the 1995 season, the sledging 'has been bad, yeah. But there's nothing you can do'.

Still there were some signs of change. In early 1995, Nicky Winmar and Dale Kickett noted that on-field racism had lessened in 1994. Yet a number of individual players, and certain clubs, remained serial offenders. And abuse from spectators remained high. In the aftermath of Winmar's gesture in 1993 the AFL had pledged to tackle the problem with an education campaign for clubs and community. But by early 1995 no such campaign had materialised. Instead, the AFL had focused on drafting a code of conduct for players and teams.

Consultation for the proposed code of conduct was intensive, with the AFL seeking input from Aboriginal players and community groups, the AFL Players' Association, clubs, and various government and legal advisory bodies at state and federal levels. By March 1995 the AFL was ready to circulate its draft. Drafted by Ron Merkel QC and AFL lawyer Jeff Browne, the blueprint addressed racism, gambling on matches, use of illegal drugs, and players who publicised injuries sustained in games or training. On the question of racial abuse, it stipulated that players shall 'not act towards or speak to any other person in a manner which threatens or vilifies that other person on the grounds of his or her race, colour or national or ethnic origin'.

The draft code of conduct sent mixed messages on racism. On the one hand, it recommended penalties for substantiated on-field racial or ethnic slurs, with suggested fines of $1000 for a first offence and $5000 for subsequent offences. On the other hand, it fell short of making racial abuse a reportable offence. Nevertheless, the code's stance against racism was widely praised by Aboriginal players and community groups. Winmar was delighted, welcoming the proposal as 'the best thing for the Aboriginal people. It's pretty helpful to us ... All we want to do is do what we are good at and play well in footy'. And once again commentators harked back to Winmar's gesture as the pivotal moment in the movement against racism in footy. But there were still questions about when and how the code would be implemented. And soon another pivotal moment would occur to test the AFL's commitment to eradicating racism.

. . . . . .

Michael Long's AFL career had almost been ruined by racism. As a young player he'd responded to abuse with his fists and by early 1993 Long was being warned by the AFL tribunal chairman regarding his 'far from impressive' record of suspensions. Essendon club president David Shaw responded by publicly decrying racism, and Long rewarded this display of support with the best season of his career. Long would also later point to the inspiration he gained from Nicky Winmar's gesture – a signal that actions and words could be more powerful than fists. 'Nicky was a leader, and we needed heroes like him to pave the way.' But when a Collingwood player called Long a 'black bastard' in front of the umpire on 25 April 1995, Long wanted action. Yet the umpire didn't report or even caution the player despite the focus on the AFL's draft code of conduct.

Like Gilbert McAdam at Victoria Park in 1993, Long's hurt and frustration were exacerbated by the presence in the crowd that day of family, in this case his brothers, Chris and Patrick. And like McAdam two years before, Long decided that it was time for a further statement. Long confronted Essendon manager Danny Corcoran in the dressing rooms immediately after the game, insisting 'I've had enough of this shit. I don't have to take it'.

On Friday 28 April 1995, newspapers broke the story that Long had been subjected to 'shocking' racial abuse by an unnamed Collingwood player. By the weekend Long had publicly identified Collingwood ruckman Damian Monkhorst as the culprit. He also repeated what was said: 'We wrestled each other to the ground near the members wing and it was while I was getting up he called me a black bastard'. Writing in his regular column – 'Long Shot' – in that week's *Sunday Territorian* in Darwin, Long described how he was 'hurt and annoyed' by the comments. 'What happened between Damian Monkhorst and myself in the last quarter was not right and something that has to be eliminated from the game.'

Long wanted an apology from Monkhorst. And as an icon and a role model for Indigenous Australians, he also aimed to test the proposed new code. In support of Long and Essendon's other Aboriginal players – like Che Cockatoo-Collins who'd also been abused racially that season – David Shaw, Essendon's president, pressed the need to act and lodged a formal complaint with the AFL on 1 May 1995.

The AFL was under pressure to respond decisively. Indigenous players, including Territorians Russell Jeffrey, Michael McLean and Maurice Rioli, spoke up, all agreeing that racism was 'definitely alive' in the AFL competition. Carlton's Craig Bradley was one of the few non-Indigenous players to argue that racism was a problem that had to be addressed by the AFL. Pressure also came from external figures. The federal Race Discrimination Commissioner, Zita Antonios, called for the introduction of a code of conduct, adding that 'sport in general needs to take account of racism'. And Senator Nick Bolkus, the federal minister for Immigration, weighed in as he had done in 1993, urging the League to investigate Long's claim and to implement a workable code of conduct.

The AFL's initial response to Essendon's formal complaint was positive. Commissioner Graeme Samuel reaffirmed the League's intention to address racism. Those who argued that on-field racism was part of the game and should be tolerated were 'living in some sort of time warp', he contended. On 1 May, the League's investigations officer, Martin Amad, began interviewing players and umpires about Long's complaint against Monkhorst. The AFL also circulated a revised draft code to clubs.

Three other Essendon players confirmed Long's story, differing only in their belief that Monkhorst had called Long a 'black cunt' rather than 'black bastard'. Yet Collingwood argued that there was no proof for Long's claim. 'There is no racism whatsoever in Collingwood', said Allan McAlister, claiming 'we are doing all we can for the Aboriginal people of Australia'. He also defended Monkhorst. 'There has been nothing proven. There is no evidence to support it.' The Magpies retained a QC, Jeffrey Sher, to act for Monkhorst, and hinted that it would take legal action against the AFL if it found the Magpie player guilty.

The litmus test for the AFL came on Friday 5 May, when it held its press conference. It was a test the AFL failed miserably. The Commission had met the previous evening to adjudicate on a number of issues. The most pressing of them all was Amad's report, and afterwards a deal was brokered between legal representatives from Essendon, Collingwood and the AFL under which Monkhorst would privately apologise to Long the following morning immediately before the press conference. In the morning, Long and Monkhorst were summoned to the AFL offices at the MCG and left alone to discuss the matter. The players duly met, but unbeknown to Ross Oakley, Monkhorst did not apologise to Long. Instead Monkhorst reportedly said, 'You took it the wrong way, mate'.

At the news conference, Oakley announced that Long and Monkhorst had settled their differences through mediation. The two had issued a joint statement, Oakley said: 'We have met this morning to discuss this issue and believe it has been satisfactorily resolved. We are not prepared to make any comment on the matter other than to say it is now behind us and we now both want to concentrate on playing good football for our clubs'. No penalty was imposed on Monkhorst. Moreover, Oakley indicated that fines for individual players would be dropped from the proposed code. 'Penalties are not appropriate in this situation', he said. 'Mediation is definitely the best way to resolve these matters and we'll be attempting to do that if any such action comes up before us in the future.' As Long fumed in silence, Oakley announced that the mediation process had led to a 'perfect solution'.

. . . . . .

The AFL had made Long 'feel like a fool', but his anger stemmed from more than just that. The League had blinked at the first sign of real opposition. Not only had Long been silenced and forced to sit through a charade of reconciliation, but the AFL had failed to penalise Monkhorst or Collingwood and then promptly abandoned its proposed penalty system. This is why Long used signs to indicate that he had been gagged and then drew his index finger across his throat.

It was a public relations disaster for the AFL. Long came out of the meeting firing, telling journalists that he was 'upset and angry' at the AFL's handling of the situation, that he had been silenced, and that he was considering suing the AFL. The only positive Long could find was that 'young [Indigenous] kids like Collingwood's Robbie AhMat know players can't do this sort of thing'. And he felt the need for the code of conduct was even more urgent, but also that it must contain strict penalties for offenders. 'I did tell Oakley that the present rules were not good enough and that I wanted harsher penalties imposed.'

Over the next few days the AFL was slammed for the way it had handled the complaint. Its process was described variously as a farce, a fiasco and bungled, while the outcome was deemed a cowardly about-face after pressure from 'white legal muscle'. For his part, Senator Bolkus claimed the AFL's 'settlement' on 5 May gave a 'yellow light' to racism in football, while story after story of the racial abuse of Indigenous footy players emerged. For many Indigenous Australians, the situation was aggravated by jokes made around the same time by Arthur Tunstall, secretary-treasurer of the Australian Commonwealth Games Association, about Cathy Freeman and Lionel Rose stealing the Pearly Gates after being barred from Heaven because they were Indigenous.

And Winmar? When the Long versus Monkhorst story broke in the press, Gary Colling, St Kilda's football manager, reported that Winmar did not want to be interviewed about the incident. According to Colling, Winmar said that if he were taunted now he would also officially complain rather than protest in the way that he had done in 1993. But Winmar did speak up after the press conference with

Long and Monkhorst. 'The AFL's handling of the issue', he said, 'had embarrassed the Aboriginal community'. Winmar felt the situation created greater uncertainty for Indigenous players. 'We don't know where we stand now. What's going to happen when it happens again? It's just sad, that's all.'

. . . . . .

Meanwhile, Long worked to ensure that the AFL developed a stronger response. That weekend he dined with Essendon coach Kevin Sheedy and president David Shaw, with Shaw subsequently noting he would approach the AFL to complain that Friday's mediation process was unsatisfactory and the code as it stood was 'toothless'. But most significantly, Long sought assistance from other Indigenous players.

Two days after the failed mediation, Essendon played the Brisbane Bears. As the players left the ground after an Essendon victory, Long approached Brisbane's Michael McLean. The captain of the Aboriginal All-Stars was a senior Indigenous player who, like Long, had come from Darwin to play footy in Melbourne before moving to Brisbane. 'It was one of the hardest things I have done', recalled Long later. 'I said, "Mick, I need your help". He was a Darwin boy and I looked up to him. It was hard for indigenous players at the time. We didn't have the answers but we knew [racist abuse] was wrong. Enough was enough.'

McLean had been inspired by Long's stance and was keen to assist him. 'I had nothing but total admiration for Long in the courage he showed to speak up. And when he was prepared to put up his hand I wanted to do the same thing. I wanted him to know that as a fellow Aboriginal I supported him 100 per cent.' Afterwards Michael McLean spoke with his team-mate Gilbert McAdam, telling him 'enough's enough. We've got to put a stop to this'. Together McLean and McAdam formulated a plan and gained support from key Indigenous players in each state.

The AFL, too, knew that it needed to redress the situation. On Tuesday 9 May they arranged a further meeting between Long and Monkhorst at which Oakley was also present. This time Monkhorst apologised after hearing how Long felt and how the abuse had hurt him. Oakley too apologised for the AFL's handling of the matter, explaining that he had genuinely believed the two players had reconciled before the Friday press conference. But an apology was only a small part of Long's agenda. At that meeting, Long restated his demand for the introduction of the long-awaited code of conduct backed by penalties for offenders. Mediation, Long argued, was not enough – 'It should be a hefty suspension and a fine as well'. And emboldened by the support of other Indigenous players, Long indicated to Oakley that the AFL needed to investigate the culture of racist abuse that remained part of footy.

Oakley agreed. The next day the AFL sent its communications manager Tony Peek to Brisbane to meet with Gilbert McAdam, Michael McLean and Darryl White. The same day the AFL finally began its long-promised community education campaign with advertisements published in the *Age* and the *Herald Sun*. The 'Changing Attitudes' ads stated: 'Racism, in any form, whether on or off the field, is totally unacceptable and will not be tolerated by the AFL Commission'. These notices also indicated the AFL's intention to promote education and mediation over penalties, and itemised four intended actions: initiating a cross-cultural training program for AFL and club personnel, encouraging clubs to do the same, developing an anti-racism advertising campaign aimed at spectators, and adopting a code of conduct.

Peek's consultation with Indigenous footballers revealed that six to eight AFL players were still routinely abusing Indigenous opponents. After speaking with McAdam, McLean and White in Brisbane, Peek began to appreciate the seriousness of the situation, with McLean telling him that he didn't want his three sons 'to follow in my footsteps if this keeps happening'. In the next few days Peek journeyed to Sydney and Perth to meet with a representative group of Aboriginal players who spoke directly with the AFL in a video-conference held on 17 May. The players – Gilbert and Adrian McAdam, Michael Long, Chris Lewis, Derek Kickett, Chris Johnson and Justin Murphy –

wanted to ensure the AFL made good on its word to act as well as speak against racism. They told the League executive that the incident with Long was 'the final straw' and that the AFL was in danger of losing Indigenous kids to sports like soccer and rugby league. Adding further pressure, Michael McLean personally threatened to name the group of racist players. 'There are a handful of them', he said, 'and if things don't soon improve I'll start identifying them. I've been silent for too long'.

The AFL responded by notifying those clubs for which the serial offenders played and announcing various training and education programs. They worked with the Victorian Aboriginal Education Association to develop a cross-cultural training program for players and staff, and on 18 May, in conjunction with the Victorian Directorate of School Education, announced a program to help prevent racism in Victorian schools. TV ads were also produced carrying the tag line 'Racism: The Game is Up'. And the AFL also advised its umpires to report incidents of racial abuse.

After two weeks of intensive consultation and announcements, it became clear that the AFL had made progress. On 12 May, AFL umpire David Ackland made a confidential report that the Melbourne player Graeme Yeats had racially abused Richmond's Indigenous player Justin Murphy. After the debacle of the initial Long–Monkhorst mediation, the AFL quietly arranged for a mediator from the Human Rights and Equal Opportunity Commission to meet with the two players. The first the media knew of it was on Thursday 18 May, the day of the meeting. If the mediation failed, the case was scheduled to be heard by the AFL Commission and possibly referred to the tribunal, but the mediation process was successful, with both Murphy and Yeats joining in a call for the AFL to 'stamp out racism in football'. The scene was now finally set for the implementation of a code of conduct.

. . . . . .

'**R**ule 30: A Rule to Combat Racial and Religious Vilification' was implemented on Friday, 30 June 1995. For the first time in a professional Australian sport, competitors were prohibited from racially abusing opponents. Or, to use the technical language of the rule, 'no player … shall act towards or speak to any other person in a manner, or engage in any other conduct which threatens, disparages, vilifies or insults another person … on the basis of that person's race, religion, colour, descent or national or ethnic origin'.

Importantly, umpires were charged with reporting instances of abuse, taking the burden away from Indigenous (and other) players to report it themselves. The new rule set in place a process of confidential mediation for disputes in the first instance, overseen by the Human Rights and Equal Opportunity Commission. If mediation failed, the complaint could then proceed to the AFL Tribunal. But despite the agitation of Long and others, players would not be fined. Instead, clubs would be liable for up to $50 000 in penalties if the complaint was proven at the tribunal. Among other strategies introduced at the time were proposals to encourage Indigenous community football development, and to fund AFL Aboriginal development and liaison officers in each state.

Aboriginal players welcomed the initiative despite the removal of fines. Long said 'It's great that the AFL has done something about it ... I'm very happy something has been done about it. It's been a long time coming'. Nicky Winmar expressed optimism. 'Hopefully it will make them [abusive players] think before they say things ... We need to wipe it out for good, cut it out for the sake of the kids.' The AFL Players' Association and football clubs also widely praised the AFL for introducing Rule 30, with even Collingwood's director of football, Graeme Allan, indicating his club's acquiescence. 'We are quite happy with it. We have no complaints, we think it's OK.'

. . . . . .

Like Nicky Winmar's statement in 1993, Michael Long's determination to pursue action revived arguments about racism in sport. Bruce Ruxton, the president of the Returned Services League (RSL), spoke for many when he likened 'black bastard' to 'dirty white bastard'. Columnist Kaz Cooke sharply countered this line of thinking:

> Michael Long comes from a place few of us can fully understand: where children were taken away from their parents because they were Aborigine, and are still lost today. Where tiny Aboriginal babies still die today of the common flu, or malnutrition. Where some men have a 20-year shorter life expectancy because they are black. Where Aboriginal women are denied health care offered to non-Aboriginal women. Michael Long comes from Australia. So being abused for being black is not the same as being called a big old handbag. It's not the same as being called porky-chops.

Long was also questioned and denigrated for his stand. When Essendon lodged its complaint with the AFL, Tony Shaw sounded a warning. 'I just hope Michael knows what he's doing. You can get a reputation ...' Historian Sean Gorman notes that many former footballers described Long as a 'trouble maker, a "jumped up" darkie who did not know his place'. And at an Essendon versus Collingwood game in August 1995, the Magpies cheer squad held aloft a banner showing a baby's dummy painted in Essendon's red and black with the slogan 'Sticks and stones may break my bones but names will never hurt me'. The banner, and Collingwood's failure to condemn it, caused a furore.

Not surprisingly perhaps, the new rule did not end either on-field racial abuse or the taunts of fans. Cultural change is difficult and racist attitudes in footy had long gone unchallenged. The AFL continued to undertake educational programs that linked into Rule 30. In the ensuing months the AFL campaigned against racism in the lead-up to the 1995 Grand Final, and appointed football development officers to work with Aboriginal communities in the Northern Territory, Queensland and Western Australia. Many of these actions were as much aimed at building bridges with Aboriginal communities as they were targeted at racism. Yet initiatives such as an ad published in the *Football Record* in 1996 indicated a willingness to continue tackling the issue – photos of Michael Long, Gilbert McAdam and Chris Lewis, and players of various migrant backgrounds, accompanied the text 'The MCG, Subiaco and Football Park. For some players they're all grounds for complaint'.

What this ad pointed to was the continued occurrence of racial abuse after the introduction of Rule 30. All up, ten complaints were lodged under Rule 30 from July 1995 to mid-1997, and there were at least fourteen reported cases of on-field racial vilification to mid-1999, all between players on opposing teams. Most were confidentially mediated, but their continued occurrence stirred the ire of key Aboriginal players. Nicky Winmar, Michael Long, Che Cockatoo-Collins, Michael O'Loughlin and Maurice Rioli all spoke up about the unacceptability of racism in sport during this period and lobbied for tougher action. Long was especially vociferous. He remained critical of apologies which did not always appear to be heartfelt, and wrote an article criticising the existing system: 'The AFL's attempts to rid football of racism have been well-intentioned, but the fact is it remains a serious problem'. In April 1997, Aboriginal players reported there were eight to ten regular offenders in the AFL, while the AFL itself acknowledged there were six.

With pressure mounting, the AFL tweaked its new code. Its new CEO, Wayne Jackson, announced in a media release late on the night of 22 April 1997 that players could bypass mediation and go directly to the tribunal. As well, the tribunal chairman, Neil Busse, warned clubs to take their player education role seriously or risk fines up to $50 000. The following week, the AFL also promised to further review Rule 30. Throughout, Aboriginal players lobbied the League for harsher penalties, including community work and mandatory education programs, even where mediation resolved a dispute. As a result, more changes were made during 1997, including allowing players at tribunal to have legal representation, mandating adoption of a uniform education program on racism for all clubs, and penalising breaches of confidentiality.

The AFL's anti-vilification rule was undoubtedly pioneering and recognised by all interest groups as a step in the right direction. It had been commended by the United Nations Association in Australia with a special peace prize, and was also copied by other Australian sporting codes. But clearly more work remained to be done.

. . . . . .

Two moments in 1997. On 27 July, Winmar played his 200th AFL game when St Kilda defeated Brisbane at Waverley. He was the first Aboriginal player to reach this career milestone. Martin Blake observed in the *Age* that the 'more confident, articulate and assured Michael Long has usurped Winmar's role as the main spokesman for Aboriginal players nowadays, but it remains a fact that Winmar started something when he lifted his jumper to a Victoria Park crowd in 1993 and proclaimed: "I'm black and I'm proud to be black"'.

On Saturday 27 September, St Kilda lost to Adelaide, 125 to 94, in the grand final at the MCG. Nicky Winmar played in that game with a heavy heart. His father, Neal, had died the day before, on Friday 26 September, in hospital in Narrogin, Western Australia. On the Thursday night, hospital TVs broadcast Channel 9's 'The Footy Show' coverage of the grand final week program from Adelaide's Flinders Park. One million TV viewers and 12 000 live spectators watched Yothu Yindi play 'Treaty' and heard Eddie McGuire, the show's host, call for an end to racial vilification in the game.

In a symbolic march for reconciliation broadcast that night, six Aboriginal players carried Australian flags and six non-Indigenous players carried Aboriginal flags. The leading players in the procession were Michael Long, who carried the national standard, and Damian Monkhorst, who held aloft the red, yellow and black Aboriginal flag. As the Winmar family bade farewell to Neal and barracked for Nicky, they knew that their son had played a pivotal role in the AFL's stance.

While racism continued to 'raise its putrid head' in the game throughout 1997 and beyond, much had occurred in the four years since Winmar exposed his skin and, in doing so, re-exposed the issues of race in Australian Rules football in 1993. A national discussion had ensued. After initial missteps the AFL had taken a proactive stance against racism. And in Rule 30 racist abuse was finally prohibited for the first time at the highest levels of Australian sport. It was not a perfect solution and Aboriginal players were unhappy with the outcomes of many of the high-profile cases. But overt racism in the game would no longer be an acceptable part of the culture.

9

The life and burdens of an iconic image

'A symbol of pride'

On Monday 20 May 2013, Nicky Winmar and Gilbert McAdam stepped out once more from the players' race onto the sodden turf of Victoria Park. Wayne Ludbey followed a few moments later, then went to fetch his camera. This time, however, the camera was just for show. For Ludbey, like Winmar and McAdam, was there as part of the AFL's 2013 Indigenous round – a round celebrating Winmar's compelling gesture just over 20 years before.

It was a typical Melbourne winter's day, the kind detested by each of these men from warmer climes. Icy rain had been teeming down all morning, reminiscent of the cold showers in the opposition rooms at Victoria Park and other suburban footy grounds. But then, after a press conference in the bowels of the ground, the rain departed, replaced by a faint sun. It is tempting to wonder what the three men saw as they gazed off into the now-empty stands.

Were they taken back to that fateful sunny day in April 1993, the stands filled with barrackers roaring for blood, the atmosphere poisonous with hate? Did their noses twitch at memories of the smell of urine and clogged toilets wafting out onto the ground as the abuse rained down? Did Winmar seek out the spot where he'd famously lifted his jumper, then blown kisses as Collingwood fans spat at him? Did McAdam search for the spot where his father had stood, then hurried out, sick to the bone at the insults directed at his son? Did Ludbey hear once again Winmar defiantly saying 'I'm black and proud', over and over again? And did the nape of Feder's neck tingle, sitting at a desk in Sydney, looking at pictures that might be placed in the *Australian* the next day?

Feder, of course, was the missing element from the gathering. Even the biggest moments, the ones that provide a fulcrum for change, don't shape the lives of all their participants equally. And while the moment of Winmar's gesture lives on for Feder, his life had taken other turns and he'd fallen out of the story. In a telling sign of the way history is created by acts of forgetting as well as remembering, Feder hadn't been invited by the AFL, and the journalists covering the story wrote of only one photographer, Wayne Ludbey.

The reverse was almost true for McAdam. In the early tellings of the story his role was considered incidental, but this gradually changed. Nevertheless, he would have more pivotal experiences of race – both public and private – than the moment captured by those photos. In contrast, both Winmar and Ludbey came to be defined by the moment and its aftermath, though not quite to the same extent. This was a cause for joy, but the moment and its reproduction also imposed various burdens on the two men. Indeed, like the iconic protest image of Tommie Smith, John Carlos and Peter Norman on the medal dais in Mexico City in 1968, at times the picture extracted a 'bitter price' for some of those involved. Never a millstone, never bringing regrets, but always packing a punch. For each of these four men it was a conduit, variously a bolthole for retreat, an avenue of painful personal discovery, a pot-holed road and a pathway for reflection on lives, pasts and careers.

. . . . . .

Sport careers are strange, fleeting things. Few other working lives are as transient. Teachers, journalists, artists, historians, photographers and most others can continue to follow a career path over decades, reinventing themselves as need be. Australian Rules football players, however, have generally retired by their mid-thirties at the latest. The kids who debut aren't thinking of this of course, but of the glory they hope to find. Both Nicky Winmar and Gilbert McAdam received more glory than most who get to play in the AFL, though neither was fortunate enough to play in a team that won a premiership. Yet if Winmar and McAdam had ever paused as kids to think about how they would bow out, it's likely they dreamed of a spectacular climax. As with most players, however, no such climax eventuated.

Winmar retired from the AFL in 1999 after an exceptional career – he'd played 251 games, kicked 317 goals, won two best and fairests, and two marks of the year, and many recieved other honours. But the ending was something of an anti-climax. At the end of 1998 he'd been delisted by St Kilda after another season full of promise had gone awry. A year after reaching the grand final, the Saints won 11 of their first 14 games to sit a game clear on the top of the ladder. But St Kilda lost their last seven, including two finals. It was a mixed season for Winmar, who was the Saints' top ball winner in their last game, a final against Melbourne, but had been disciplined by the club late in the season after a match in which he repeatedly clashed with Carlton tagger Anthony Franchina. Dismayed by the run of defeats, St Kilda sacked coach Stan Alves, and the new coach, Tim Watson, elected not to renew the 33-year-old Winmar's contract.

Winmar was drafted by the team that St Kilda had battled for top position for much of the 1998 season, the Western Bulldogs. Almost immediately he found himself at the centre of another furore. In early 1999 Winmar cancelled an appearance on Channel 9's 'The Footy Show'. Controversial panellist Sam Newman responded by blackening his face and pretending to be Winmar on national television, making jokes about 'going walkabout' with host Eddie McGuire looking on. Newman did it for laughs but Winmar was deeply offended and hurt, for the tradition of 'blackfacing' is a demeaning one that is again tied to notions of racial inferiority. (White performers would put black shoe polish on their faces and then sing and act in a child-like manner.) Winmar and Newman went through a confidential mediation process which led to Newman apologising, but Newman promptly called the process a 'charade', undoing any of the goodwill that his apology might have provided.

The incident overshadowed an impressive season by Winmar, whose precise disposal, versatility, runs and goal kicking helped the Bulldogs back into the finals. But then on a cold windy evening at the MCG, Winmar injured his leg in the opening moments of the Dogs' first final against West Coast. The Bulldogs lost narrowly, and Winmar missed the ensuing finals defeat to an emerging Brisbane Lions team. Although he had another year left on his contract, Winmar did not feel up to another pre-season and retired in November 1999.

Many lamented Winmar's departure, with tributes flowing in from around the nation. He was celebrated for his brilliant play and tireless running, but most pieces inevitably turned to focus on his 1993 gesture of pride and defiance. The *Koori Mail* attributed the sadness of Indigenous people at his retirement to the 1993 image: 'It all stems, of course, from "that photo"'. But soon that photo would weigh on Winmar's heart. Not because he regretted his action – far from it. Rather, it conferred on him a special responsibility to explain his action, prove his meaning, repeatedly discuss it, and in many ways become a spokesman for Aboriginal rights in and out of sport.

. . . . . .

In his own way, Gilbert McAdam had already become a spokesman and activist for Aboriginal rights in the early 1990s. Unlike Winmar, McAdam hadn't had negative experiences of race as a kid, but that had only intensified the shock of the abuse he experienced when he moved to Adelaide. He knew it wasn't right and developed a thick skin to cope. But McAdam was also happy to speak out and push for change, as he did when chatting with journalist Caroline Wilson before the finals in 1991.

While at St Kilda, McAdam studied at Monash University, learning about *terra nullius* and the enduring struggles of Indigenous Australians for freedom, equality and land. The realisation that the 1967 referendum on Aboriginal rights occurred in the year of his birth was a revelation for the young footballer. The High Court's Mabo decision and Paul Keating's Redfern Address were 'emotional times'. McAdam took these lessons into his work as the AFL's inaugural Aboriginal liaison officer, helping instil pride and resilience and battling to put teeth into the AFL's code of conduct. Yet in late 1995 Gilbert McAdam realised that he knew little of his family's own history and struggles. It was a moment that reshaped his life.

As he grew older, Gilbert's father, the normally taciturn Charlie McAdam, decided to tell his story to the world. Maybe his distressing experience in the crowd at Victoria Park had shown him that the angry white spectators needed to learn where their hateful attitudes came from, or maybe it was the feeling that his time in this world was coming to an end. Regardless, he enlisted the help of the writer Elizabeth Tregenza to help chronicle the remarkable life he and the rest of his family had lived. The result was the publication in 1995 of a ground-breaking book, *Boundary Lines*, that told compelling tales of theft, abuse, survival and rebuilding two years before the Australian Senate would release *Bringing Them Home*, their report into the Stolen Generations.

Reading the book, Gilbert learnt for the first time of Charlie's experience being 'civilised' by beatings and deprivation at Moola Bulla station and his mother Val's experience of being taken away to be 'looked after' in Adelaide. For the first time Gilbert could understand his father's hard, ruthless edge. Suddenly, Australian Rules football did not seem so important. Instead, Gilbert felt a hunger to know more, to find his place in relation to his heritage. At the end of the 1995 season he journeyed to the Kimberley in Western Australia to start meeting and reconnecting with his father's side of the family.

The process affected Gilbert deeply. On one visit to Halls Creek he was overcome by the emotional reception given him by local people, who cried and hit their heads with stones. On another trip, with athlete Nova Peris, he was so overwhelmed by emotion during a school visit that he couldn't speak to the children and had to sit down.

At the end of the 1996 AFL season, Brisbane offered Gilbert McAdam a generous two-year contract. He didn't take it up. 'I wanted to go back and follow my roots and find out more stuff about my father.' Just as a camera had exposed racism in football, a video-camera helped McAdam uncover his roots. In the period before his father died, Gilbert McAdam filmed all of the significant sites he could in Halls Creek, the tree which the child Charlie had clung to in desperation to avoid being stolen, the landscape, the places of dreaming. And he met his father's stepfather, an elderly man named Yunguntji, who had helped raise the young Charlie and taught him the ways of the land. Now when his children come of age, Gilbert can help them connect to their heritage.

After Charlie McAdam died, Gilbert returned briefly to football, re-signing to Central District in the South Australian National Football League for the 1998 season.

More recently he has returned to footy via the media, commentating for the National Indigenous Radio Service and co-hosting 'The Marngrook Footy Show'. To both he brings a deep knowledge of the trials, traumas and triumphs of Indigenous Australians – and an awareness of the need to mark and tell this history – along with an ability to play the clown as well as anyone.

......

L ike Gilbert McAdam, John Feder also left the world of Australian Rules football, albeit a little later and for different reasons. Sports photography had been fun, and the Winmar gesture was one of a number of great pictures he'd taken. Others included Sydney forward Warwick Capper's famous mark over Hawthorn's Chris Langford during the 1987 qualifying final, and Carlton star Stephen Silvagni's 'mark of the year' in 1998. Most notably, in 1994 Feder captured another indelible Australian moment of race and sport, taking the celebrated photo of a jubilant Cathy Freeman holding the Aboriginal and Australian flags on the running track in Victoria, Canada, after her 400 metres victory in the Commonwealth Games. Again, it was an image that sparked debates over racism in sport and race in Australia.

But back then Feder wasn't so 'into the more serious issues'. This changed in the late 1990s when he took up a series of overseas assignments for the *Australian* that led to intense adventures of their own. In 1999, Feder was sent to East Timor, where he spent two three-month stints with the pro-independence movement. He was in Dili when the East Timorese voted overwhelmingly for independence and thus bore witness to the horrifying retribution enacted by the Indonesians. It was not the last time Feder found himself at a scene of great trauma. In 2000, Feder became the chief photographer for News Limited. Based in Canberra, he travelled extensively and was with Prime Minister John Howard in Washington DC on 11 September 2001 when terrorists crashed their hijacked plane into the Pentagon. He and the Howards were on their way to a press conference when secret service staff started running around like crazy, saying that a plane was headed for the White House, 300 metres up the road.

In the Iraq war that soon followed, Feder slipped across the border into Iraq from Kuwait with journalist Peter Wilson. They filed some amazing stories before being arrested at gunpoint by Iraqi officers and taken off for questioning. Feder thought 'they were going to take us out the back and shoot us. But incredibly they didn't'. Instead they were driven through the war zone to Baghdad. 'We saw tanks exploding and all this scary stuff.' In Baghdad, Feder and Wilson were kept under house arrest. They were still under house arrest in a Baghdad hotel a few weeks later when the US army advanced on the city. A US shell hit the hotel, killing two people on the floor above them. 'It was just madness.'

Feder was glad to escape the madness and return to Sydney, where he became a picture editor for the *Australian*. And although he has dropped out of the story of the Winmar image, Feder has found his thoughts returning to that time. Even though the image didn't define him it remains close to his heart, and he's often congratulated when people discover he took it. In late 2012, perhaps in preparation for the 20th anniversary of the moment, Feder printed out a large copy and hung it in his house. After two decades it is now a scene he sees daily.

. . . . . .

The Winmar image never left Wayne Ludbey. Unlike Feder, Ludbey had heard Winmar saying 'I'm black and I'm proud to be black'. Pictures might be worth a thousand words, but these words became synonymous with the image. Ludbey was just trying to do his job to the best of his ability, to capture the moment as accurately as possible. Yet in reporting what Winmar said, he was putting his credibility on the line. And 'all you've got in this game is credibility'.

The burden on Ludbey's shoulders would have been eased if Winmar had come out and confirmed that what Ludbey had heard was correct. But Winmar had been gagged by St Kilda, and even in later years the club remained uncomfortable with him speaking about racism and thus distracting from their core business of winning games of football. And a troubling counter-tale emerged over time that Winmar had actually been pointing to his stomach, not his dark skin, and telling the crowd that he 'had guts'.

It was a strange interpretation, based on the *Herald-Sun*'s second attempt to interpret the image that day (their first edition had Winmar saying 'How good am I?') – strange because the people arguing for it were somehow implying that Winmar wasn't responding with defiance and pride to racist abuse. As if that abuse hadn't pushed him to the point of wanting to make a statement that would end it all. As if the controversy that followed was due to a misunderstanding of the image, with the implication that Nicky Winmar shouldn't be credited with a major intervention against racism in Australian Rules football. Yet Winmar's general silence on the issue gave the interpretation some credence, and each time someone put it forward it was like they were saying Wayne Ludbey had got it all wrong.

Whenever Ludbey ran into Winmar there was 'real warmth', but never the chance to discuss the moment in any detail. A story circulated that Winmar had privately denied it. So despite the warmth, Ludbey was 'haunted for years' by the possibility that Winmar might back away from the comments that Wayne had relayed to his editors and the public. 'I used to actually stay awake at night fucking worrying that Nicky was just going to come out and say "you know, it's totally been misconstrued". It just used to really stress me out.'

Ludbey's fears were based in part on the lowly position that photographers occupied in the hierarchy within newspapers. 'For a photographer to actually say, "this is what I heard, this is what he did", it was fairly unusual. And I'm easily discredited, aren't I? "Oh, he's the fucking snapper", or "what does he know, those blokes can't even spell".' But Ludbey had also developed a reputation as a trouble-maker. Often it came through in the jovial slaps from journalists accompanied by proclamations that 'here comes trouble'. But sometimes there seemed to be a more sinister edge to it. On one occasion Ludbey's father was 'bailed up at a party' and grilled about the Winmar incident and told, 'You know, your son is causing trouble'. Ludbey also received occasional letters of hate-filled abuse, calling him an Aboriginal sympathiser or accusing him of having Indigenous blood himself, as if there was something wrong with that.

But at times the image also felt like it 'saved' Ludbey as well. The dark moments when he questioned his career were inevitably interrupted by someone telling him just how important his photograph of Winmar's gesture was – that the image had changed their life, that they'd never seen something so inspiring, that he was a hero in Central

Australia. Ludbey would realise then how amazing it was to have taken such a critical photo while simply doing his job. And he remained forever grateful that he'd helped the world bear witness to Nicky Winmar's 'incredible courage'. Still, it was a great relief when Ludbey finally found out that Winmar had publicly confirmed his words at that moment (something that Winmar has done many times now).

. . . . . .

It seems, at times, that Nicky Winmar is still waiting for his moment of relief. He's proud of his gesture and words, and happy to be a poster boy in the literal sense, with his photo up in lights. He's even re-enacted the gesture on rare occasions. But the shy and taciturn former footballer was reluctant to be a poster boy in the flesh, to be called upon as a leader and to speak about racism in footy over and over again.

Winmar hasn't completely shunned public roles. He carried the Olympic torch in 2000, has participated in sport and cross-cultural programs, and has also been an active figure in community anti-violence programs. But he's also needed time 'to find himself', time to seek healing and 'in many ways, acceptance'. It takes a lifetime, perhaps more, to deal with growing up in 'a state of near apartheid'. And Winmar still has 'a lot of hurt, yeah. Probably anger as well. We do keep those things inside ourselves'.

Football was a place of escape, of dreams and joy. But the abuse of opponents and spectators would take that away. People want Winmar to return to the moment of his gesture because they often see it as a moment of triumph. Yet for Winmar it remains a moment of trauma. There he was with Gilbert McAdam, two Indigenous men playing football near land which had been sacred to the traditional custodians of the area. And instead of being celebrated or judged for their deeds on the field, they were being constantly denigrated in a way that evoked the pain of his history, of what had been done to him and his people.

It's little wonder, then, that at times Winmar has sought to escape the constant questions about that moment and the memories they bring. He and his partner Beth have often destroyed the sim cards of their mobile phones and changed their phone numbers in the hope that they can live without the constant calls to speak out again. At the press conference for the AFL's 2013 Indigenous round, Winmar admitted that he initially didn't want to come to Melbourne for it. When a journalist asked him why, Nicky responded with a question of his own: 'Have you ever been to Pingelly?' 'No' replied the journalist, and soon the conversation moved on to other matters. But it is the forgotten history of 'attractive' towns like Pingelly that lies behind Winmar's gesture.

Like many former athletes, Winmar is haunted by the loss of the game he loves. He often dreams that he's back playing footy, running, kicking and leaping high. It's hard enough for athletes to move from the world of physical play with its powerful bodies and honed skills to the world of words and memories. When all these words constantly take you back to moments of trauma, it is harder still.

. . . . .

It's not easy, either, being cast as a villain in a story that people continually retell. As central figures in the tale, Tony Shaw and Damian Monkhorst have also carried their share of burdens over the past two decades. Every Anzac Day reminds Monkhorst of the abuse he directed at Michael Long when wrestling with him on the wing in their encounter in 1995. He says his one-off, 'heat-of-the-moment' comment was a 'huge mistake'.

Shaw, who infamously told Caroline Wilson in 1991 that he'd willingly make a racist comment on the field if he thought he could get away with it, has never named the number of times he played the racist card in his career. With hindsight he admits that 'I was naive and I was wrong'. He received death threats, but what disturbs him the most is being called a racist.

With some justification, both Monkhorst and Shaw are aggrieved for being singled out for blame when the problem of racism was rampant throughout football culture. Yet 20 years on, they have largely reconciled, happy to 'carry the can' for their roles in the dramas highlighting the extent of that problem and leading to its clean-up.

. . . . . .

In April 2013 the National Sports Museum in Melbourne opened a special exhibition titled 'Black and Proud: A Stand Against Racism' to mark the 20th anniversary of Nicky Winmar's protest gesture at Victoria Park. Wayne Ludbey brought his proud parents to the launch, which featured his never-published sequence of photographs of Winmar immediately before, during and after the incident. Like a time-lapse study of a butterfly chrysalis, they show the famous gesture in its phases of emerging and departing. Of course the central image has never left us, but has morphed into a ubiquitous cultural symbol. And right on cue, when Nicky Winmar and Gilbert McAdam reunited in Melbourne the following month for the 2013 AFL's Indigenous round, new street art – a larger-than-life paper cut-out of Winmar's 1993 pose – appeared overnight on Trenerry Crescent next to Victoria Park.

The power of the Winmar image was obvious at the 'Black and Proud' exhibition. Renditions included the Ludbey and Feder prints, the Peter Nicholson and Rocco Fazzari illustrations, paintings by Indigenous artists Hudson Dinah and Dan Kelly, works by street artists like Regan Tamanui (aka HaHa), and the fourth National Aboriginal and Torres Strait Islander Sports Awards poster from 1993. These items were a mere representative sample of the broad raft of reproductions available, chosen and curated to highlight the impact of Winmar's gesture on sport and in popular culture. The larger, uncurated trove of Winmar-inspired paintings, book covers, graffiti, street art, cartoons, physical emulations and re-enactments that exist throughout the country attests to the appeal of the gesture and the power of its meaning. Their impact has repeatedly elevated the image to most-popular polls. It ranked first of 150 photos in a public poll conducted by the *Sunday Herald Sun* in 2008 to determine football's greatest image. Along with the Kennedy assassinations and Princess Diana's funeral, it scaled the shortlist of the most memorable press photos nominated by *Sunday Age* readers in 2000, and ranked high in a 2005 listing of the most iconic sports photos of all time.

The distillation of these ubiquitous images reminded the four key protagonists – Winmar and McAdam, Ludbey and Feder – of their roles and their contributions. As Winmar and McAdam attended media rounds during the AFL's Indigenous round, giving interviews and reflecting on 1993, they came face to face with photographic reminders of that transformative moment. Winmar expressed pride in his action and was 'heartened' to see the AFL taking a harder line against racism. McAdam wished he'd been a part of it. At the exhibition launch, the sparkling lights made Ludbey's eyes water in pride. And every day as Feder comes home from work he smiles at the print of his photograph hanging in his hallway. Yet it remains an image born out of trauma – a defiant statement of pride and an enduring demand for change.

Epilogue

It seemed like an awful parody. The AFL's 2013 Indigenous round was not supposed to turn into another scandal around racist abuse. Not after a week celebrating the 20th anniversary of Nicky Winmar's compelling gesture. Not with the most senior, celebrated Indigenous man currently playing AFL being vilified by a kid and denigrated by an AFL club president within three days. And yet here we somehow were, with Adam Goodes first called an 'ape' and then linked to King Kong.

No footy picture taken in the last twenty years has spoken to racism as powerfully as the image of Winmar pointing in pride and defiance to the colour of his skin. But the image of Adam Goodes responding to the call of 'ape' came closest. It was late in the opening match of the 2013 Indigenous round. Adam Goodes, starring for Sydney against Collingwood, kicked the ball forward from the wing. His momentum took him along the boundary fence, then suddenly he turned around, drew the attention of a security guard, and pointed to the girl who had just unwittingly vilified him. Captured from behind by AFL photographer Andrew White, Goodes is statuesque in profile, as if he was intentionally embodying the latest campaign against racial vilification: 'Racism. It stops with me'.

Speaking to the media the next morning, Goodes admitted that he was 'gutted'. 'How could that happen?' he asked. 'This week is a celebration of our people and our culture.' Goodes had had the 'privilege of meeting Nicky Winmar two days ago' and felt that in pointing out this latest instance of racism he was following in Nicky's footsteps. But the abuse had taken him back to high school where he was bullied with endless taunts along the lines of 'monkey' and 'ape' on account of his skin colour. Goodes hoped that the kid and everyone else would learn that these comments didn't just hurt him, they hurt his brother, mother, family, and 'all black people everywhere'. It was hundreds of years of painful history that made such 'a simple name, a simple word, cut so deep', and the Australian people needed to understand how hurtful it was.

Collingwood president Eddie McGuire seemed to understand all this. He'd been left ashen-faced by the incident and was the first person to go into the Sydney rooms after the game and apologise to Goodes. Yet less than a week later, McGuire suggested that Goodes should promote a new stage show of King Kong. Goodes was flabbergasted, McGuire ashamed. But initially at least, McGuire didn't seem to understand just why his attempt at humour was so offensive and said he didn't know where his reference to King Kong had come from.

The two instances provided a revealing insight into just what has and hasn't changed in the 20 years since Winmar had made his famous gesture. The girl who vilified Goodes was promptly escorted by security out of the MCG. The actions might have been heavy-handed, but it was a clear sign that racist abuse by spectators was no longer tolerated. A year earlier, Collingwood player Dale Thomas had gone as far as pointing out a Collingwood barracker who was racially abusing his opponent, Joel Wilkinson, an act celebrated as symbolising the end of racism in Australian Rules football. Yet not only were moments of abuse continuing to occur, much of the public response to the denigration of Goodes was disturbing. Many people simply didn't understand why he was so offended and advised him of the need to harden up and deal with such trivial insults.

The lesson unintentionally provided by former Collingwood president Allan McAlister had been forgotten – the public link between racist abuse and the history of damaging assumptions of Indigenous inferiority had been lost. And not for the first time. Indeed, what struck us in researching the history and impact of Nicky Winmar's gesture is just how frequently key moments in the struggle for Indigenous rights featured on the front pages and then disappeared from public memory. Somehow there was no enduring story of Australia's highly problematic race relations for these moments to become part of.

The photos of Winmar are an intriguing exception. Australian Rules football is the language of much of Australia. What happens on footy ovals at the elite level is likely to be remembered, debated and told over and over again. And Winmar's stunning statement brought race into the heart of this conversation. The power of the image facilitated important change. But for the underlying causes of racism to be addressed, we need to begin remembering more than just Winmar's gesture.

In the aftermath of Goodes's vilification, Jason Mifsud, the AFL's head of diversity, made a critical point. Unconscious biases and assumptions reveal themselves in moments of rage and attempts at humour. The enraged call of 'ape' and supposedly humorous joke about King Kong both pointed to the assumptions promulgated by the long-discredited science of race. Both were deeply offensive because they link back to a history of discrimination and violence that was justified by claims that Aboriginal peoples were lesser humans. Yet this history remains largely neglected outside of universities and Indigenous communities.

Not only do we need to know about Nicky Winmar's gesture of pride and defiance, we also need to know more of the history of settlements like Pingelly and of the lives of people like Sir Doug Nicholls, and Charlie and Val

McAdam. These are not only tales of discrimination, but also of resistance, power, pride and triumph. Until they are remembered, Australian Rules football, and Australian society more generally, will remain a site of unwitting, as well as witting, expressions of racism. It's hard to think of a more compelling justification for the importance of history.

Artist Hayden Dewar painted the Nicky Winmar gesture as part of his mural of the history of Melbourne on the wall of Dimmeys in Richmond.

Acknowledgments

This book has been a labour of love and we are indebted to the many people who have helped to sustain, support and guide us. First of all we would like to thank those who agreed to be interviewed for this book: Nicky Winmar, Gilbert McAdam, Wayne Ludbey, John Feder and so many more. We feel privileged to have been trusted with such compelling and often intimate memories – your voices are the heart of this tale and we hope that our history illuminates and does justice to your stories.

Like so many others, historians build on the foundations laid by those who laboured before us and we owe particular thanks to the vital work of Colin Tatz, Henry Reynolds, Charlie McAdam, Elizabeth Tregenza, Barry Judd, Quentin Beresford, Greg Gardiner, Lawrence McNamara and Sean Gorman. Sean was also a marvellous supporter and mentor who encouraged us right from the start and helped us maintain faith in our vision for this book through to the end. Other key guides included Paul Stewart, Ciannon Cazaly, Jason Oakley and Tony Birch. We are also very thankful for the support provided to this project by Uncle Kevin Coombs, Ian Anderson, the AFL Players' Association (and especially in this regard to Nadia Taib and Kelly Applebee), and to Adam Goodes for his kind words. And then there is our wonderful and formidable fellow traveller, Tim O'Brien, whose support and energy has been a blessing.

The National Sports Museum and Melbourne Cricket Club more generally provided a glorious base for much of the research for this book and the associated exhibition. Our deepest thanks go to the grand staff at the Museum and the MCC Library, with special mentions to Helen Walpole, Jed Smith, Margaret Birtley, Sarah Gordon, David Studham and Trevor Ruddell, whose personal newspaper clippings were a treasured resource. We are also thankful for the excellent research assistance provided by Jordy Silverstein and Jess Coyle, to the National Library of Australia's superb Trove digital collection, for the aid from Ashley Humphrey, and to Sam Brooks for his work on the index.

We have both been blessed with an amazing collection of colleagues at Victoria University and the University of Queensland who have helped to nurture and inspire our research, though we can only mention a few by name: Jessica Carniel, Clare Hanlon, Dennis Hemphill, Jackie Huggins, Teresa Kaczynski, Dominique Lanuto, Doune Macdonald, Louise McCuaig, Brent McDonald, Michael McKenna, Fiona

McLachlan, Sue Monsen, Deb Noon, Rebecca Olive, Terry Roberts, Tony Rossi, Maureen Ryan, Steven Rynne, Caroline Symons, Richard Tinning, Melissa Walsh, Hans Westerbeek, and especially our inspiring fellow sport historians and mentors, Rob Hess and Murray Phillips.

It has been a true pleasure to work with NewSouth on this book and we are especially grateful to Phillipa McGuinness and the inestimable Emma Driver. Sue Harvey was an excellent editor and we are very thankful to Roger Franklin for earlier editorial assistance. Sophie Cunningham, John Hirst and Alex McDermott provided invaluable help in setting this book on the path to publication. Alex was also a valued proofreader and thought-provoking conversationalist among many other fine things. Robin Murphy and Barbara Jennings likewise provided vital insight and ongoing research support. Peter Nicholson and Rocco Fazzari generously gave permission for the use of their brilliant cartoons, while John Feder, Roger Hyland, Emile Andrew and the Australian Football League kindly provided photographs. We would also like to thank Codie Madden from AFL Photos, Marilia Ogayar from Newspix, Peter Lindeman from Fairfax and the librarians at the State Library of Victoria, University of Queensland and Victoria University.

Finally, this book would not have been possible without the incredible support of our beloved friends and families, and we're especially grateful to have Fiona Kerr, Hannah Klugman-Kerr and Freya Klugman-Kerr, and Anthony Bartolo, Willa Basset and Jeanie Basset in our lives.

References

All quotes from Nicky Winmar, Gilbert McAdam, Wayne Ludbey and John Feder are from our interviews with them in 2012 unless otherwise noted. The references that follow are grouped together according to the subsections in each chapter.

Epigraph

Nelson Mandela commented on the inspirational power of sport in a speech in Monaco on 25 May 2000 when he presented Brazilian footballer Pele with the inaugural Laureus Lifetime Achievement Award. Author Steve Hawke called Nicky Winmar's 1993 gesture 'the AFL's Rosa Parks moment' in 'My joy, the magic of the red-dirt footballer', *Age*, 20 February 2010, 'Sport', p. 10.

Prologue

The tale of Charlie McAdam is drawn from his book with Elizabeth Tregenza (1995) *Boundary Lines*; and the *Herald Sun* 'Weekend', 5 August 1995, pp. 4–5. Gilbert McAdam detailed some of the racial abuse directed at him in *Boundary Lines*, p. 192. Other taunts are discussed in the *Age*, 20 April 1993, p. 1; and 24 April 1993, p. 1; and *Herald-Sun*, 26 April 1993, p. 19. The land title for Tanami Downs, the Northern Territory station where Charlie was once head stockman, was handed back to its traditional owners on 21 December 1992.

1 Agitating for change

The National Film and Sound Archive has Ron Casey's call (and a partial transcript) of the 1968 world bantamweight title fight between Lionel Rose and Masahiko Harada. General details about Rose were drawn from Colin

Tatz (1987) *Aborigines in Sport*, and the *Advertiser* (Adelaide), 14 May 2011. Descriptions and quotes of the fight and its aftermath are from *Sports Illustrated*, 24 June 1968; *Age*, 13 May 2006, p. 12; and *Age*, 1 March 1968.

Quotes on the history of Pingelly are from the websites Australian Explorer <australianexplorer.com/pingelly.htm> and Shire of Pingelly <pingelly.wa.gov.au>. Descriptions and quotes about the Pingelly reserve are from *West Australian*, 17 July 1970, p. 7; and 28 July 1970, p. 6; and Quentin Beresford (2006) *Rob Riley*, pp. 59–63. Winmar made the comment about growing up in Pingelly to the *West Australian*, 21 July 1999, p. 153.

James Stirling's report and letter to Governor Darling is reprinted in Malcolm Uren (1948) *Land Looking West*. Further details on Stirling and the Swan River Colony are from the profile of him in the *Australian Dictionary of Biography*. Stirling's proclamation of the new colony can be found at the Museum of Australian Democracy website <foundingdocs.gov.au/item-sdid-7.html>, while the orders to establish a 'Superintendent of Natives' and mounted police corps are at Find & Connect Western Australia, <findandconnect.gov.au/wa/biogs/WE00494b.htm> and <findandconnect.gov.au/wa/biogs/WE00564b.htm>.

The 'Batman Land Deed' (and transcript) can be found on the National Museum of Australia's website, which also notes John Batman's claim to be the 'greatest landowner in the world'. Governor Bourke's proclamation can be viewed at the Museum of Australian Democracy website, <foundingdocs.gov.au/item-did-42-aid-8-pid-73.html>. Batman's letter to Thomas Anstey is detailed in Alastair Campbell (1987) *John Batman and the Aborigines*. George Arthur's quotes concerning Batman are from the profiles of Batman on the National Museum of Australia website and in the *Australian Dictionary of Biography*.

Yagan was described as a hero by the *West Australian*, 17 June 2010 and a 'complete and untameable savage' by Robert Dale (1834) *Descriptive Account of the Panoramic View, &c. of King George's Sound, and the Adjacent Country*, p. 15. The encounter of George Fletcher Moore and Yagan is from *Perth Gazette and Western Australian Journal*, 1 June 1833, p. 87. Yagan's capture and time with Robert Lyon is detailed in Henry Reynolds (1998) *This Whispering in Our Hearts*. The corroboree, attack, subsequent bounty and Yagan's murder are recounted in the *Perth Gazette and Western Australian Journal*, 16 March 1833, p. 42; 4 May 1833, p. 71; and 20 July 1833, p. 114.

Sean Gorman (2011) commented on the silence concerning the 1868 tour in 'A whispering', in Christian Ryan (ed.) *Australia: Story of a Cricket Country*, pp. 128–35. The quotes from JG Wood and William South Norton are from David Sampson (2009) 'Culture, "race" and discrimination in the 1868 Aboriginal cricket tour of England', *Australian Aboriginal Studies*, vol. 2009, no. 2, pp. 47, 45. Baldwin Spencer (1914) made his comments in *Native Tribes of the Northern Territory of Australia*.

The *Australian Women's Weekly* profile of Doug Nicholls was published on

12 June 1957, p. 18. Details of the Yorta Yorta are from Wayne Atkinson (1996) 'The Yorta Yorta struggle for justice continues', in Greta Bird, Gary Martin, Jennifer Nielson (eds) *Majah: Indigenous Peoples and the Law*, pp. 281–9. The 'Invincibles' are profiled on the Rumbalara Football & Netball Club's website, <rumba.org.au/history. html>. Further details on Nicholls, including the Melbourne *Herald* headline, are from Andrew Ramsey (1998) 'Sir Douglas Nicholls', in Colin Tatz et al., *AFL's Black Stars*, pp. 27–33; and Mavis Thorpe Clark (1975), *Pastor Doug*. The celebration of Nicholls's play as a 'brilliant wingman' is from the *Sydney Morning Herald*, 15 August 1931, p. 17; the *Argus* profile is from 21 June 1934, p. 7S; and Nicholls's awareness of the way members of the Yorta Yorta followed his progress is from the *Albany Advertiser*, 24 June 1935, p. 4. Details about William Cooper are from Bain Attwood and Andrew Markus (2004) *Thinking Black*. The speeches from the Day of Mourning were printed in the *Australian Abo Call*, 1 April 1938, p. 2. Nicholls's reference to sport as his 'university' is from the *Australian Women's Weekly* profile, while his aim to raise the status of 'all Aborigines' is from *Thinking Black*, p. 10.

The ban on Indigenous footballers was reported in the *Mail* (Adelaide), 24 October 1953, p. 4S; *West Australian*, 11 April 1950, p. 5; and *Argus*, 17 October 1953, p. 44. The desire for clarification over the definition of 'native' was reported by the *West Australian*, 19 November 1954, p. 10.

The Pingelly school strike was reported in the *West Australian*, 2 December 1942, p. 2. For more on the Progress Association see the *West Australian*, 18 July 1949, p. 16. Resistance to the new housing funded by the Western Australian Government was also reported in the *West Australian*, 3 December 1954, p. 8.

The Freedom Ride is detailed in Ann Curthoys's (2002) book *The Freedom Ride*. The 1963 Yirrkala bark petition can be seen at the Museum of Australian Democracy website <foundingdocs.gov.au/item-did-104.html>. The Wave Hill 'walk-off' is detailed by the National Archives of Australia at <naa.gov.au/collection/fact-sheets/fs224.aspx>. EO Lange's comments were reported in the *West Australian*, 19 August 1967, p. 8.

For more on Peter Norman see Matt Norman's (2008) film *Salute*, produced by Wingman Pictures.

2 Growing up in different Australias

Winmar detailed the way he and his partner regularly changed their phones in the *Herald Sun*, 29 June 2010.

Winmar's terror of cricket is from his profile in Sean Gorman (2011) *Legends*, p. 126. Details of the 'speccy' practice is from the *Sunday Herald* (Melbourne), 31 March 1990, while the wet grounds are noted in Gorman's *Legends*.

The tale of Charlie McAdam is again drawn from McAdam and Tregenza (1995) *Boundary Lines*, and the *Herald Sun* 'Weekend', 5 August 1995, pp. 4–5.

The story of Richard Cotter is drawn from our interview with him in 2012.

WEH Stanner made his lament about the 'Great Australian Silence' in his 1968 Boyer Lectures. These are published in his (1969) book *After the Dreaming*.

3 Formative moments

Details of anti-apartheid protests are drawn from Jennifer Clark (1998) '"The Wind of Change" in Australia', *The International History Review*, vol. 20, no. 1, pp. 89–117. The quote from Bradman is in the *Sydney Morning Herald*, 23 August 2008, p. 29. Bradman's reluctance to cancel the tour was detailed by Trevor Grant in 'Cricket and racism still a potent partnership' on his blog *What's the Score, Sport?*, 13 November 2012, <wtss.com.au/?p=75>.

Jennifer Clark's quote and related details are in the aforementioned 'The Wind of Change', p. 116. The Naomi Shannon quote is from her 2004 article 'The Friendly Games?', in Ian Warren (ed.) *Buoyant Nationalism*, p. 48. The Dawe poem is 'Watching the '82 Games' in his (1986) collection *Towards Sunrise*. Winmar's regard for Benny Vigona is detailed in *Westside Football*, 18 July 1985, p. 7.

Winmar's performances in 1982 were reported in *Southscene* (South Fremantle Football Club), March 1982, p. 16; July 1982, p. 8; and November 1982, pp. 6, 20. The recruiting visit of Bulldog players and officials is from *Westside Football*, 31 March 1983, p. 20; and the *West Australian*, 17 March 1997, p. 5. Winmar noted his surprise to the *Western Mail Weekend*, 19–20 April 1986. His pre-season form excited reporters from *Westside Football*, 31 March 1983, p. 20; and the *Daily News* (Perth), 30 April 1987. Colin Tatz (1987) detailed both the vilification of Evonne Goolagong and the Ella brothers (and Mark's comparison to South Africa) in *Aborigines in Sport*. For more on racism and Australian Indigenous athletes, see: Sean Gorman (2005) *Brotherboys*; Barry Judd (2008) *On the Boundary Line*; and Colin Tatz (1995) *Obstacle Race*. The racial abuse of West Indies cricketers is documented in Stevan Riley's (2010) film *Fire in Babylon*. Syd Jackson wrote his comments about racism in the *Age*, 11 April 1993, 'Sport', p. 17. Winmar's commitments outside of football are covered in the *South Fremantle Year Book 1983*; *Westside Football*, 18 July 1985, p. 7; and the *Western Mail Weekend*, 19–20 April 1986.

The quotes from Greg McAdam and Elliot McAdam are from McAdam and Tregenza (1995) *Boundary Lines*, pp. 179–84.

Details for Winmar's first season are from the *Football Budget* (WA), 6 June 1983, p. 25; and the *West Australian*, 27 May 1983, p. 59; 30 May 1983, p. 64; and 7 June 1983, pp. 90–2. The quotes for his second season are from *Westside Football*, 18 July 1984, p. 7; and 24 April 1984, p. 24; and the *Football Budget*, 28 April 1984. The turmoil of the 1985 and 1986 seasons is from the *Western Mail*, 15–16 February 1986, p. 98; *Westside Football*, 18 July 1985, p. 7; *West Australian*, 2 May 1985; *West Australian*, 19 June 1986; *Daily News*, 30 April 1987; *Daily News*, 31 July 1986; *West Australian*, 12 July 1986; and *Daily News*,

2 May 1985. The circling of VFL clubs was reported in the *Football Budget*, 28 April 1984. Essendon's interest is from the *West Australian*, 21 July 1999; and the *Sunday Age*, 5 September 1999, p. 15. The story of St Kilda's recruitment and Winmar's adjustment to Melbourne is detailed in the *Sunday Herald* (Melbourne), 31 March 1990. Abblitt's quote was from the *Daily News* (Perth), 30 April 1987.

Claremont's recruitment of Gilbert McAdam is from *Westside Football*, 3 April 1986, p. 14.

Information on the Barunga Statement can be found at <www.aiatsis. gov.au/collections/exhibitions/treaty/barunga.html>. The quotes and details from Caroline Martin are drawn from our interview with her in 2012. Henry Reynolds's encounter with the soapbox speaker in London is described in his (1999) book *Why Weren't We Told?*, p. 23.

The reaction of the McAdam family to Gilbert winning the Magarey Medal is from McAdam and Tregenza (1995) *Boundary Lines*, pp. 185–6. The response to Gilbert McAdam's discussion of racial abuse is from the *Sydney Morning Herald*, 10 October 1989, p. 4.

Brereton's column was in the *Sunday Age*, 12 August 1990, 'Sport', p. 3. The frustrations of Winmar are detailed in the *Sunday Age*, 12 August 1990, 'Sport', p. 15; and the *Age*, 13 August 1990, p. 30. Brereton admitted to abusing Winmar in the *Age*, 18 August 1998. Winmar's apology was reported in the *Age*, 17 August 1990, p. 26; while the reference to the Yellow Pages is from the *Sunday Age*, 19 August 1990, p. 32.

4 Rising concerns

The details of Caroline Wilson's conversation with Gilbert McAdam and associated investigation into racism in the AFL are from our interview with her in 2012. Wilson's report of racism in the AFL was published in the *Sunday Age*, 25 August 1991, p. 6.

The hate campaign against young Indigenous players was detailed by Wilson in the aforementioned article. The story of Chris Lewis is from the biography on him in Gorman's *Legends*, pp. 133–140. Derek Kickett's comment was reported in the *Age*, 30 April 1995; and Danny Ford's recollections are from the *Age*, 17 May 1994, p. 7. Malthouse wrote about Lewis in the *Australian*, 16 September 2011. Martin Flanagan's comment is from the *Koori Mail*, 10 August 2005, p. 75. Details of the Lewis–Viney encounter are from the *Age*, 12 July 1991, p. 26; and Wilson's article. The price gouging of fans was reported in the *Sunday Age*, 14 July 1991, p. 1. News of the HIV tests appeared in the *Age*, 16 August 1991, p. 24.

Stephanie Holt's quote is from her excellent (1999) essay, 'Go Nicky', in Peter Craven (ed.), *The Best Australian Essays 1999*, p. 239. Bill Deller's comment is from Wilson's aforementioned piece on racism in the AFL. The letters to the editor are from the *Age*, 29 August 1991, p. 12; *Sunday Age*, 1 September 1991, p. 14; and *Sunday Age*, 8 September 1991, p. 14.

Brereton's apology to Chris Lewis was reported in the *Age*, 16 September 2011. Lewis detailed his disappointment in the *West Australian*, 16 September 2011. The Cook comments were from Wilson's aforementioned report on racism in the AFL.

For more on Yothu Yindi and 'Treaty' see Aaron Corn (2009) *Reflections and Voices*. The comments and details about Paul Stewart are from our interview with him in 2012.

The description of the mid-season Collingwood versus St Kilda game is from the *Sydney Morning Herald*, 9 June 1992, p. 42. The details and quote for the 1992 Collingwood versus St Kilda final are from the *Sydney Morning Herald*, 7 September 1992, p. 26.

Keating's Redfern Address can be found on the *australianscreen* website, <aso.gov.au/titles/spoken-word/keating-speech-redfern-address/extras/>. The emphasis in the text is ours. The *Age* editorial is from 5 April 1993, p. 11. The unforgettable speeches voted by ABC Radio National listeners can be found at <www.abc.net.au/rn/features/speeches/>. The recollections of Caroline Martin are from our interview with her in 2012.

The incident between Worsfold and Long was later pinpointed as the moment 'the football racism issue is [on its way]' by the *Sunday Age*, 26 September 1993, p. 4. Worsfold's denial was reported in the *Sunday Age*, 25 April 1993, p. 3. Shaw's presidential speech was detailed in the *Sunday Age*, 4 April 1993, 'Sport', p. 3. The *Sunday Age* called racism 'Football's black mark' on 11 April 1993, 'Sport', p. 2. Syd Jackson's piece was in the same edition, p. S17.

5 The match

Gilbert McAdam's description of the abuse he and Winmar faced is from the *Herald Sun*, 29 June 2011; McAdam and Tregenza (1995) *Boundary Lines*, p. 192; and our interview with him in 2012.

Paul Stewart's recollections are from our interview with him in 2012, as are Troy Austin's recollections. 'Danny Boy' spoke of his memories from the game to ABC Radio's Melbourne station 774 on 14 May 2012. The 'horrified and scared' St Kilda barracker was reported in the *Age*, 24 April 1993, p. 1. The recollections of Andrew Jackomos are from our interview with him in 2012.

6 The gesture and the photos

The tale of Jesaulenko's almost missed mark is from the *Herald Sun*, 3 September 2012.

The 'statement of presence' is from David McNeill (2008) '"Black Magic"',

Race & Class, vol. 49, no. 4, p. 29. The recollections of Joy Damousi, Andrew Jackomos, Jess Roberts and Paul Stewart are from our interviews with each of them in 2012.

The recollections of Nick Place are from our interview with him in 2012. Bruce Guthrie detailed his memories in a column for the *Age*, 26 May 2013. The *Sunday Age*'s initial use of the photographs, together with the caption and story, are from 18 April 1993, p. 1.

The quotes from Lyall Corless are from our telephone interview with him in 2012. The *Sunday Herald-Sun*'s initial use of the photographs, together with the caption and story, are from 18 April 1993, p. 1.

7 The response

The recollections of Caroline Martin in this chapter are from our interview with her in 2012. Waleed Aly's story is from a piece published on the AFL website on 19 March 2008 (the piece is no longer available, but is archived at <www.aussiemuslims.com/forums/archive/index.php/t-22714.html>). The Nick Bolkus speech was reported in the *Australian*, 20 April 1993, p. 5. The initial response of the AFL was reported in the *Age*, 20 April 1993, p. 1. The same issue of the *Age* reported the silencing of Winmar and McAdam, p. 38.

Gerard Wright's report is from the *Sydney Morning Herald*, 19 April 1993, p. 34. Syd Jackson's argument for a code of conduct was in the *Sunday Age*, 11 April 1993, p. S17. Garry Linnell's comment is from the *Age*, 19 April 1993, p. 27. The *Age* editorial was from 20 April 1993, p. 15; Patrick Smith's commentary was in the same edition, p. 1, and this piece reprinted the Tony Shaw quote from Caroline Wilson's earlier article in the *Sunday Age*, 25 August 1991, p. 6. The Nicholson cartoon was in the *Age*, 20 April 1993, p. 15.

The recollections of Joy Damousi are from our interview with her in December 2012. The letters supporting Winmar's action were in the *Age* on 20 and 21 April 1993; and the *Herald-Sun* on 22 and 24 April 1993. The 'furious' Collingwood fans were reported in the *Age*, 24 April 1993. The reports of racial abuse from the next weekend's footy matches are in the *Sunday Age*, 25 April 1993, p. 3, and the *Herald-Sun*, 28 April 1993, p. 18. The Mary Millard quote is from the aforementioned *Sunday Age* report. Allan McAlister's initial dismissal of the abuse is from the *Age*, 20 April 1993, p. 1. Simon Madden's column was in the *Age*, 22 April 1993.

McAlister's comments were reported in the *Age*, 26 April 1993, p. 1.

The responses of Syd Jackson and Robert Nicholls are from the *Age*, 26 April 1993, pp. 1, 4; while that of Moira Rayner is from the *Age*, 27 April 1993, p. 4. The Rocco Fazzari cartoon was published in the *Sunday Age*, 9 May 1993, p. 15. McAlister's apology to Nicholls was detailed in the *Age*, 27 April 1993, p. 1, as was the general apology from Tony Shaw. The announcement from the AFL was reported in the *Age*, 28 April 1993, p. 36. The 'goodwill' tour was deemed a 'circus' in the *Age*, 16 May 1993, p. 15. McAlister's reception in the Northern Territory was detailed in the *Sydney Morning Herald*, 11 May 1993, p. 4. See the *Age*, 16 May 1993, p. 15, for an example of the way the protest by Victorian delegates was dismissed.

Adrian McAdam's delight at seeing the Aboriginal flag was reported in the *Sunday Age*, 30 May 1993, p. 1. The same piece reported McAlister's comment that 'we've had enough'. Details of the Collingwood versus West Coast game are from the *Sunday Age*, 27 June 1993. The recollections of Paul Stewart are from our interview with him in 2012.

Mick McGuane's comments were reported in the *Sunday Age*, 29 August 1993, p. 9. The appointment of Gilbert McAdam's as AFL Indigenous liaison officer was detailed in the *Age*, 14 July 1993, p. 34.

As is tradition, the 1993 AFL grand final poster was also the cover of the grand final *Football Record*, 25 September 1993. The details of the grand final entertainment are from this edition of the *Football Record*. Michael Long's dream of winning the premiership in the International Year of the World's Indigenous People was reported in the *Age*, 27 September 1993, p. 3.

The fourth National Aboriginal and Torres Strait Islander Sports Awards were reported in the *Age*, 4 November 1993, p. 32. The recollections of Andrew Jackomos are from our interview with him in 2012.

8 The next step

Wayne Ludbey's photo of the press conference with Michael Long, Damian Monkhorst and Ross Oakley was published in the *Herald Sun*, 6 May 1995, p. 1.

Paul Keating's comments are from the *Age*, 12 February 1994, p. 7, and the *Sunday Age*, 13 February 1994, p. 1. Daniel Lewis's piece was published in the *Sydney Morning Herald*, 10 February 1994, p. 11 and detailed the responses of both Robert Tickner and Gary Colling. The *Sunday Age* front page is from 13 February 1994, p. 1. Leigh Matthews's quote was on this front page, while Michael McLean's quote was in the *Age*, 14 February 1994, p. 28. Allan McAlister's comments were reported in the *Age*, 11 February 1994, p. 34.

Che Cockatoo-Collins spoke about the racist abuse he received on a number of occasions including those reported in the *Age*, 17 May 1994, p. 7; 30 April 1995, p. S2; and 2 May 1995, p. 54; and *Herald Sun*, 11 March 1995, p. 93. The comments from Nicky Winmar and Derek Kickett noting the reduction of racist taunts are from the *Koori Mail*, 22 March 1995, p. 24; and the *Herald Sun*, 11 March 1995, p. 93. The initial failure of the AFL to mount its promised education campaign against racism was reported in the *Age*, 8 May 1995, p. 1.

For more on the draft code of conduct see Greg Gardiner (1997) *Football and Racism*, p. 4. The reactions to the draft code are drawn from the *Herald Sun*, 11 March 1995, p. 93; the *Koori Mail*, 22 March 1995, p. 24; and the *Age*, 30 April 1995, p. S2.

REFERENCES

Details of the warning to Michael Long concerning suspensions are from the *Age*, 22 April 1993, p. 26. Long celebrated Winmar's leadership in a column for the *Age*, 18–19 April 2003, p. S5. Long's statement to Danny Corcoran is detailed by Michael Winkler (1998) in '1993–98: The AFL and the fight against racism', in Colin Tatz et al., *AFL's Black Stars*, p. 99. For one of the first stories regarding the vilification of Long see the *Age*, 28 April 1995, p. 1. Damian Monkhorst was identified as the culprit by Long in the *Northern Territory News*, 29 April 1995, pp. 1–2; along with the *Age*, 29 April 1995, p. 1; and *Sydney Morning Herald*, 8 May 1995, p. 45. Long expressed his distress at the comments in the *Sunday Territorian*, 30 April 1995, p. 39. Long's aim to test the new code was reported in the *Sydney Morning Herald*, 8 May 1995, p. 45, while David Shaw's actions are detailed in the *Age*, 29 April 1995, p. 1 and over the ensuing days. The pressure on the AFL from Indigenous players and Craig Bradley was detailed by the *Northern Territory News*, 29 April 1995, pp. 102–104. The additional pressure from external figures was reported in the *Age*, 1 May 1995, p. 4. The response of the AFL is from the *Age*, 2 May 1995, p. 54; and 3 May 1995, p. 34; and the *Herald Sun*, 6 May 1995, p. 94. The confirmation of Long's claim by three other Essendon players was reported by the *Sydney Morning Herald*, 8 May 1995, p. 41. Collingwood's response was covered in detail by the *Age*, 30 April 1995, p. 1; along with the *Northern Territory News*, 4 May 1995, p. 36; and 5 May 1995, p. 38. The deal between legal representatives was noted by the *Age*, 4 May 1995, p. 36, with the same paper reporting Monkhorst's statement that Long had taken his comment 'the wrong way' on 10 May 1995, p. 48. Oakley's quotes about the mediation are from the *Australian*, 6–7 May 1995, p. 1; and the *Northern Territory News*, 6 May 1995, p. 70.

Long's sense that the AFL had made him 'feel like a fool' was reported in the *Northern Territory News*, 6 May 1995, pp. 1, 70, with his comments to Oakley reported in the later edition of the paper on 10 May 1995, p. 56.

The AFL was slammed in the *Australian*, 6–7 May 1995, p. 1; and 8 May 1995, p. 32; in the *Age*, 6 May 1995, p. 36; 8 May 1995, p. 1; and 23 June 1995; and in the *Herald Sun*, 6 May 1995, p. 94. The Arthur Tunstall joke was reported in full by the *Sunday Territorian*, 21 May 1995, p. 17. Gary Colling claimed that Winmar did not want to be interviewed in the *Age*, 30 April 1995, p. S1. Winmar's statement after the AFL press conference was reported in the *Herald Sun*, 6 May 1995, p. 96.

Shaw's comment that the draft code of conduct was 'toothless' is from the *Australian*, 8 May 1995, p. 32. Long's comment that approaching McLean 'was one of the hardest things I have done' was made to the *Herald Sun*, 29 June 2011, p. 1. McLean's admiration for Long was reported by the *Sunday Age*, 3 September 1995, p. 15. Gilbert McAdam recollected McLean saying to him 'enough's enough' in our interview with him in 2012. The second meeting between Long and Monkhorst was detailed by the *Northern Territory News*, 10

May 1995, p. 56. Long's demand for penalties was reported in the *Age*, 10 May 1995, p. 48. The first AFL anti-racism advertisement in the *Age* was on the same page. The consultation by Tony Peek, along with Michael McLean's comments about his sons, were reported in the *Herald Sun*, 29 June 2011. Details of the teleconference and associated quotes by Long and McLean are from the *Sunday Territorian*, 14 May 1995, p. 7. The AFL's multi-pronged response was reported variously in the *Australian*, 6–7 May 1995, p. 2; and 19 May 1995, p. 22; in the *Age*, 13 May 1995, p. 24; 17 May 1995, p. 38; and 18 May 1995, p. 36; and the *Football Record*, 2 July 1995, p. 3. The call by Justin Murphy and Graeme Yeats to 'stamp out racism in football' was detailed in the *Age*, 20 May 1995, p. 38.

The full text of Rule 30 was printed in the *Football Record*, 2 July 1995, p. 19. The response of Long, Winmar, the AFL Players' Association and Graeme Allan is drawn from the *Herald Sun*, 1 July 1995, p. 109.

Bruce Ruxton's comments were reported in the *Sunday Age*, 14 May 1995, p. 2; with Kaz Cooke's response printed in the next edition of the *Sunday Age*, 21 May 1995, p. 2. The warning by Tony Shaw was detailed in the *Age*, 5 May 1995, p. 28. Sean Gorman's report of the way many former footballers described Long as a trouble-maker is in his (2010) essay 'Sporting chance', *Cosmopolitan Civil Societies Journal*, vol. 2, no. 2, p. 15. The Collingwood 'sticks and stones' banner was reported by the *Age*, 15 August 1995, p. 28. For an example of the furore created by the banner see the *Age*, 29 August 1995, p. 32. For details of the way the AFL continued to campaign against racism see Gardiner (1997) *Football and Racism*, p. 19. The 'grounds for complaint' ad was printed in a number of editions of the *Football Record*, for example 6–8 September 1996, p. 15; and 16–19 May 1997. For details of the fourteen mediated complaints of racial vilification see Lawrence McNamara (2000), 'Tackling racial hatred', *Australian Journal of Human Rights*, vol. 6, no. 2, p. 4. For the frustrations of leading Indigenous players see, for example, the *Herald Sun*, 23 April 1997, p. 80; the *Age*, 24 April 1997, p. B8; and Gardiner (1997), *Football and Racism*, p. 23. Long's article criticising the mediation process was in the *Age*, 23 April 1997, p. B16. The continued taunts from regular offenders were discussed in the *Herald Sun*, 23 April 1997, p. 80. The tweaks to Rule 30 were reported in the *Age*, 24 April 1997, p. B8; 25 April 1997, D3; and 1 August 1997. The United Nations Association prize was reported in the *Football Record*, 2 July 1995, pp. 3, 19.

Martin Blake's comments are from the *Age*, 25 July 1997, p. D10. Descriptions of the 1997 Grand Final entertainment are from Lawrence McNamara's (1998) essay 'Long stories, big pictures', *The Australian Feminist Law Journal*, vol. 10, p. 107; and (2000) 'Tackling racial hatred', p. 13.

The *Herald Sun* referred to racism raising its 'putrid head' on 23 April 1997.

9 The life and burdens of an iconic image

The 'bitter price' quote is from the title of a piece on the 35th anniversary of the Black Power salute in the *Sydney Morning Herald*, 17 October 2003.

Sam Newman's comment that the mediation with Winmar was a 'charade' was quoted in the *Daily Telegraph*, 19 May 1999, p. 66. The *Koori Mail* lamented Winmar's retirement on 17 November 1999, p. 40.

For an example of the counter-tale that Winmar was saying he 'had guts' see the *Sunday Age*, 13 January 2008, p. S6.

For examples of Winmar re-enacting his gesture see the *West Australian*, 18 April 2000, p. 79; the *Koori Mail*, 3 May 2000, p. 1; and 1 June 2005, p. 67; and the *Sunday Herald Sun*, 24 May 2009, p. S32. Winmar's public profile since retiring is detailed in the biography on him in Gorman's (2011) *Legends*; and the *Herald Sun*, 29 June 2010, pp. 16–17. Winmar's quote about the pain of his experiences is also from the *Herald Sun* profile. Winmar's question to the journalist about Pingelly is drawn from our transcript of the 2013 AFL Indigenous round press conference.

Damian Monkhorst detailed the burdens of being a villain to the *Herald Sun*, 22 April 2011; while Tony Shaw reflected on being naive and wrong in the *Age*, 20 April 2013.

The results from the *Sunday Herald Sun* poll of Australian Rules football's greatest image were published on 4 May 2008. Results from the *Sunday Age* poll of memorable press photos was published on 25 June 2000, p. 16; while results from that paper's poll of iconic sports photos was published on 17 April 2005. Winmar noted that he was 'heartened' to the *Australian*, 20 May 2013.

Epilogue

The match between Collingwood and Sydney took place on 24 May 2013. Goodes's press conference the next day can be viewed on YouTube at <www.youtube.com/watch?v=XyrbUiJCkVw>. Jason Mifsud tweeted his comment about unconscious biases and assumptions revealing themselves in moments of rage and attempts at humour on 30 May 2013.

Image credits

Picture section

Nicky Winmar, 1992 –
Photographer: Unknown. Image
courtesy of the AFL.

Gilbert McAdam, 1992 –
Photographer: Unknown. Image
courtesy of the AFL.

Wayne Ludbey – Photographer:
Cameron Tandy. Image courtesy of
Newspix.

John Feder – Photographer:
Unknown. Image courtesy of John
Feder.

Winmar, 1993, by Feder –
Photographer: John Feder. Image
courtesy of Newspix.

Winmar, 1993, by Ludbey –
Photographer: Wayne Ludbey.
Image courtesy of Fairfax
Syndication.

Sunday Age cover – Image courtesy of
Fairfax Syndication.

Herald-Sun cover – Image courtesy of
Newspix.

Nicholson cartoon – Image courtesy
of Peter Nicholson, <www.
nicholsoncartoons.com.au>.

Fazzari cartoon – Image courtesy of
Rocco Fazzari.

Press conference – Photographer:
Wayne Ludbey. Image courtesy of
Newspix.

Canada Lane graffiti – Photographer:
Roger Hyland. Image courtesy of
Roger Hyland.

McAdam and Winmar –
Photographer: Michael Willson.
Image courtesy of the AFL.

Adam Goodes – Photographer:
Andrew White. Image
courtesy of the AFL.

Other images

Rumbalara kids – Photographer:
John Woudstra. Image courtesy of
Fairfax Syndication.

Dimmeys mural – Photographer:
Emile Andrew. Image courtesy of
Emile Andrew.

Football Record, 2 July 1995 – Image
courtesy of the AFL.

Index

$1.50

FOOTBALL RECORD

RACISM

The game's up

FITZROY
v HAWTHORN
Round 13, July 2, 1995

MATTHEW KLUGMAN researches and teaches in the history of sport in the College of Sport and Exercise Science, Victoria University. His research interests include those who love and hate sport, and the intersections of sport, race, passions, bodies, gender, sexuality, religion and migration. In 2012 Matthew was the inaugural Research Fellow of the National Sports Museum and a recipient of an Australian Research Council DECRA (Discovery Early Career Researcher Award) Fellowship.

GARY OSMOND is senior lecturer in sport history in the School of Human Movement Studies, University of Queensland. His research interests include race and sport, with a focus on Indigenous Australians and Pacific Islanders. He has received research funding from the Australian Institute of Aboriginal and Torres Strait Islander Studies (AIATSIS) and is currently a chief investigator on an ARC Linkage research project on the Australian Paralympic movement.